I HATE TO COOK!

FOR PEOPLE WHO HATE TO COOK BUT LOVE TO EAT

Ed Dugan

COPYRIGHT© 2017

ALL RIGHTS RESERVED

NO PART OF THIS BOOK MAY BE REPRODUCED OR TRANSMITTED IN ANY FORM OR BY ANY MEANS, ELECTRONIC OR MECHANICAL INCLUDING PHOTOCOPYING, RECORDING OR BY ANY INFORMATION STORAGE AND RETRIEVAL SYSTEM WITHOUT THE EXPRESS PERMISSION OF THE AUTHOR IN WRITING.

AN IMPORTANT MESSAGE FROM ME TO YOU

A very fine lady named Peg Bracken wrote a similar book, with the same title, about 50 years ago and I thought it was time for an updated look at the subject.

First, I am a professional chef who has owned several very successful restaurants, so I know whereof I speak. Although we have to eat to sustain life, nowhere is it written that you must love to cook. This cookbook has only one purpose: to get you in and out of the kitchen as quickly as possible, with the least amount of effort, but with a very tasty dish or dishes. It's my way of keeping you out of the fast food restaurants and putting on unwanted weight.

It's a proven fact that if we don't like doing something, we're not likely to be good at it. If you aren't sure about hating to cook, try reading my book, *The Fundamentals of Cooking*, which you can find on Amazon. If you want to learn more about it go to my webpage: **eddugansbooks.com**

To get ready, I would suggest stocking up with a good supply of cream of chicken, mushroom, and celery soups, diced tomatoes, canned potatoes, along with a few cans of cheese soup, and most of all, a large supply of paper plates.

There is one over-riding theme you should keep in mind. When in doubt – go out and buy it! For example, I could give you several wonderful recipes for cornbread, but why go to the trouble of making it from scratch? Either buy a packaged mix or buy it already made. It won't be as good for you as made-from-scratch food, but it will shorten your time in the kitchen.

There aren't a lot of recipes in the book because we didn't want you to get the feeling you were stuck in some sort of culinary study-hall. If you need something fast and easy, read on, and we promise no hall monitors will bother you. Many of these recipes are slightly unusual, which might help entice you into the kitchen.

Ed Dugan

TABLE OF CONTENTS
WELCOME TO THE WORLD OF THE CULINARY DISINTERESTED

APPETIZERS — PAGE

Chef Dugan's All-Purpose Appetite "Wheter" — 14

SOUPS

Cheeseburger Soup	17
Cream of "you name it" Soup	19
Cream of Black Bean Soup	21
Easy Chicken Noodle/Matzo Ball Soup	23
Chilled Borscht with Boiled Potato	25
Lentil/Split Pea Soup	26
Taco Soup	28

SALADS

Combination Salad	31
Black-eye Pea Salad	32
Waldorf Salad	34
Fastest Salad on the Planet	35
Chef Ed's All-American Potato Salad	36

Vegetables in Sour Cream Salad	38
Chef Ed's Salad Supreme	39
Fruit Salad with Chef Ed's' Dressing	41
Mediterranean Artichoke Salad	42

SANDWICHES

Paper-thin Grilled Cheese Sandwich	45
Philly Cheese Steak Sandwich	46
A Guide to Making Great Hamburgers	48
The Oklahoma Onion-Fried Burger	50
"Iowa Skinny" Sandwich	51
The Reuben Sandwich	54
Cream Cheese & Olive Sandwich	56
The Ultimate Tuna Salad Sandwich	58

EGGS

The World's Easiest Egg Salad	61
Chef Ed's Frittata	62
Huevos Rancheros	64
Tomato & Cheese Strata	65
Chef Ed's "Triple B" Cowboy Breakfast	67
Fried Eggs Spanish Style	69

Deviled Eggs	71
A Basic Recipe for Quiche	72

MAKING A SAUCE

Three Easy Steps to Sauce Making	76

BEEF

"Stuff" on a Shingle	81
Chef Ed's Special Beef Stew	83
Irish Pot Roast	85
French Poached Beef Tenderloin	87
Swiss Steak	90
Country Fried & Chicken Fried Steak	93
Carpetbag Steak	96
Steak Au Poivre	97
Quick & Easy Fajitas	99
Corned Beef & Cabbage Dinner	101
Picadillo	103
Chef Ed's Meatloaf/Stuffed Peppers	105
Liver & Onions	108

PORK

Monte's Ham	111

Last Meal Pork Chops	115
Firehouse Pork Chop Casserole	117
Bavarian Pork & Sauerkraut	119
Stuffed Spareribs	121
The Planet's Best BBQ Ribs	122

LAMB

French Leg of Lamb	125
Grilled Butterflied Leg of Lamb	128

POULTRY

The Best Way to Roast a Chicken	131
Quick& Easy Fried Chicken & Creamed Gravy	133
King Ranch Chicken	135
Breaded Lemon Chicken Breasts	138
Roast Chicken with Garlic	140
Chicken Enchiladas or Burritos	142
Grilled Tandoori Chicken with Indian Salad	145
Cheez-It Chicken	149
Roasted Chicken & Vegetables	149

FISH & SHELLFFISH

Shrimp Creole	152

Shrimp & Grits	154
Shellfish Dump	156
Fish Filets with Lemon-Butter & Caper Sauce	158
Poached Fish Filets with Tomatoes	160
Chef Ed's Crab Cakes	162
Scallops Poached in White Wine	164

RICE

Rice Tortillas	167
Company Rice	169
Low Country Rice	172
Red Beans & Rice	174
Hoppin' John	176

DUMPLINGS

About Dumplings	178

PASTA

Saucing & Other Pasta Suggestions	179
Fettuccine with Shrimp & Vegetables	182
Spaghetti Casserole	184
Noodle Pudding (Kugel)	186
Easy Lasagna	188

Macaroni & Cheese	190
Spaghetti with Fresh Tomato Sauce	191

VEGETABLES

Bubble & Squeak	194
Super Easy French Fries	195
Smashed Roasted Potatoes	196
"Pan Browned" Potatoes	198
Colcannon	199
Hasselbach Potatoes	201
Scalloped Potatoes in Cream	203
Fried Tomatoes with Tomato Cream Gravy	205
Sautéed Broccoli & Garlic	207
Incredible Baked Beans	208
Vegetable Fritters	210
Sweet Potato & Banana Casserole	213
Green Beans & Cashews in Brown Butter Sauce	215
Harvard Beets	216
Creamed Carrots & Mushrooms in a Dill Sauce	217

OTHER STUFF

Chef Ed's "Kiss My Ass" Chili	220

Cincinnati Chili	223
Bread Pudding	224
Chocoholics Heaven	226
Frito Pie	227
A Ploughman's Lunch with Pub Onions	228
Popovers	230

APPETIZERS

Chef Dugan's All-Purpose Appetite "Wheter"

Appetizers are supposed to get you in the mood for eating or, as the gourmets are fond of saying, "whet your appetite."

If that's the case, start with something "whet" like beer, wine or whiskey. Here's a drink I invented, and I guarantee, a couple of these, and you will absolutely LOVE your kitchen.

As for the rest of the appetizers, just go to the grocery store, buy a dip and some crackers, put them on paper plates and serve.

For 3 People

1 small can of frozen limeade

1 can of beer

Your choice (scotch, bourbon, rum)

2 cups ice cubes

Rocks or Margarita glasses

In a blender, pour in the can of limeade, the can of beer, the contents of the empty limeade can be filled to the brim with the liquor of your choice, and 2 cups ice cubes. Blend well until the ice is small. Pour into glasses and serve.

SOUPS

CHEESEBURGER SOUP

What could be easier than a liquid cheeseburger? This recipe includes potatoes but if you want to try a special touch, buy some store-bought French fries, pop them in the oven, and use them to dip in the soup while you're enjoying it.

NOTE: In the Vegetable Section, there's a recipe for Super Easy French Fries that you should check out.

For 3-4

1 pound ground beef

1 medium onion, chopped

3 carrots, shredded

3/4 cup diced celery

1 teaspoon dried parsley flakes

2 cans diced potatoes

1 small jar diced pimentos

2 cans beef broth

1/2 cup all-purpose flour

1 package (16 ounces) Velveeta process cheese, cubed

1-1/2 cups whole milk

Salt and Pepper to taste

¼ cup sour cream (optional)

Put the ground beef in a deep pot and cook over medium heat until brown. Add the onions, carrots, celery and canned potatoes. Cook for 3 minutes, add the flour, stir and cook for another 3 minutes. Add the beef broth and stir well. Add the milk and cheese, pimentos with their juice, and cook over low heat until the cheese has melted, and the soup has thickened. There you have it! The soup should be nice and thick but if it gets too thick just add some more broth or water.

If you want to add a dollop of sour cream before serving the soup, please do so, although cheeseburgers usually don't come with that option.

Now, if you decide to leave the potatoes out and do the French fries, buy a package a put them in the oven and serve. If you want to put a personal touch on the fries, buy a few Russet potatoes, peel and cut them into wedges, toss with olive oil and roast them in a 375 oven for 45 minutes.

CREAM OF "YOU NAME IT" SOUP

If you're REALLY watching the calories, this is the soup for you. Why, you might ask? Because it contains almost zero fat, that's why. However, if calories are not your concern, just add a cup of heavy cream or half and half and make it REALLY rich.

It can become an entire meal with some nice French bread and a salad.

For 3-4

1 cup chopped sweet onion

2 tablespoons butter

4 cups canned chicken broth

½ cup uncooked rice

Sauté the onions in the butter, over medium heat, until they are soft but not browned. Add the rice and continue to cook for 2 minutes. Lower the heat, add the chicken broth and cook for 20 minutes or until the rice is very tender. Puree the mixture in a blender or food processor until it's smooth and creamy and return to the pot.

Now you can get creative. You can add cooked broccoli, zucchini, carrots, cauliflower, green beans, mushrooms, or whatever strikes your fancy. This is also the time to add the cream or half and half. It's perfectly okay to use canned vegetables. Once the soup is made no one will ever know the difference. Do not allow the soup to boil.

CREAM OF BLACK BEAN SOUP

Although I think black beans are better suited for this soup, I've also used black-eyed peas and white beans as well. If you want to lower the calorie count you can skip the cream and the soup is still delicious.

For 2-4

1 can black beans

¼ cup heavy cream

1 jalapeno pepper, seeded and chopped

1 small onion, chopped

1 can chicken broth

1 teaspoon cumin or chili powder

1 squeeze of lime juice

Salt and pepper

Combine all the ingredients in a blender and blend until smooth. Heat until just simmering and add the cream. Stir and remove from heat.

At this point you can either serve the soup, or chill it and serve it cold. It's also very good without the cream addition.

I like to serve it with warm corn tortillas and store-bought coleslaw. Talk about easy!

EASY CHICKEN NOODLE or MATZO BALL SOUP

You should understand, no self-respecting Jewish person would ever serve this soup. Maybe a Palestinian, but not a Jew.

I grew up in a neighborhood that had a huge Jewish population and I know what I'm talking about. On the other hand, if you or your guests are not connoisseurs of Jewish penicillin, as real chicken soup is sometimes called, no one will ever know the difference.

This is good with saltines crumbled into it, or some crusty bread on the side. Bagels spread with sour cream are nice as well.

For 2-4

1 carton chicken soup (or 4 cans)

3 carrots, peeled and cut into 1" pieces (or just buy a can of chopped carrots)

1 large sweet onion, chopped (or a packaged of chopped onions)

1 sweet red pepper, chopped

3 stalks celery cut into 1" pieces

1 rotisserie chicken

Package fine egg noodles or matzo ball mix

Pour the soup into a large pot, add the celery, onion, carrots and sweet pepper and simmer for about 20 minutes.

Either shred, chop or use whole pieces to add chicken to the pot, heat for 10 minutes and serve.

If this whole process took more than 30 minutes you must have gotten distracted.

CHILLED BORSCHT WITH A BOILED HOT POTATO

If you've never had much exposure to Jewish or Russian cuisine, you probably never heard of Borscht and maybe ought to skip this recipe. On the other hand, if you're feeling bold and experimental, give it a try.

The borscht can be found in jars in any supermarket and it's nothing more nor less than a beet-based soup made with beef shanks to give it more flavor.

It's served chilled with a hot, boiled potato placed in the middle of the bowl. Most of the time it's topped with a large dollop of sour cream. Once you've tried it you'll no longer feel sorry for Russian peasants. The entire cooking time is whatever it takes to boil the potato until its done.

For 2-3

1 jar of borscht

1 potato for each person

Sour Cream

LENTIL or SPLIT PEA SOUP

There's hardly any difference between these two soups, but in any case, use dried peas or lentils and the soup will be done in about 30 minutes.

They both go well with a ham or grilled cheese sandwich. Or a grilled ham AND cheese sandwich for that matter. If you do that you can skip the hot dogs. Unless, of course, you want to serve the soup with hot dog sandwiches. Decisions, decisions.

For 2-3

2 cans chicken broth

4 cups water

1 lb. of either lentils or split peas

2 carrots cut into ¼-inch dice

1 sweet onion halved and sliced very thin

1 clove garlic, minced

2 stalks celery, cut into thin pieces

2 hot dogs or polish sausage cut into ¼-inch slices

Salt and pepper

Put all the ingredients except the hot dogs/Polish sausage into a pot and bring to a boil. Cover loosely and simmer for 30 minutes.

Pout about 3 cups of the soup into a blender and blend for one minute. You're doing this so the soup won't separate.

Return the blended soup to the pot and add hot dogs/sausage, if that's what you've decided upon. WOW – was that easy or what?

TACO SOUP

If you're only going to have one soup in your repertoire, this is it. It freezes well and is easy to make, provided you have an electric can opener. It also allows you to become as creative as you wish.

Once the soup base is made, you can add some chopped some onions, sweet peppers, jalapenos, a can or beer or a glass of wine, and even a can of cheese soup. Let your imagination run wild!

My wife loves it with a bowl of tortilla chips and a dollop of sour cream on top. You also might think of serving a packaged salad on the side.

For 4-6 or more

1 ½ pounds of ground beef

Package of dried Taco Seasoning mix

Package of dried Ranch Dressing mix

1 can beef broth

1 can diced tomatoes

1 can Rotel tomatoes (mild or hot – your call)

1 can whole kernel corn

1 can chili beans in sauce

1 can pinto or black beans

Brown the ground beef in a large pot for about 10 minutes. About halfway through, add the Taco and Ranch Dressing mixes. This will prevent the beef from clumping.

Add the rest of the ingredients, stir well and simmer for about 20 minutes. Turn the heat down to very low and serve it whenever the spirit moves you.

SALADS

COMBINATION SALAD

This is from a remarkable cookbook called ***White Trash Cooking*** by the late Ernest Matthew Mickler. In addition to some great recipes it has a centerfold of some down-home scenes you really should see.

The salad couldn't be easier to make and only has three ingredients: a head of iceberg lettuce, a few nice ripe tomatoes and plenty of mayo.

I don't mean to insult you, but this is the way you prepare a head of lettuce for a salad: First, hit the stem end hard on a counter to loosen the core and pull it out. Then let some cold water run into the lettuce to clean it out well. Finally, sit it in the sink, stem end down and let it drain. After a few minutes, shake some more excess water out of it, wrap it in 2-3 paper towels, and let it sit in the fridge to crisp up.

When you're ready to serve, chop up the lettuce into 2-inch pieces, chop up the tomatoes into 1-inch pieces and toss everything together with plenty of mayo and salt and pepper. What's not to like?

BLACK-EYED PEA SALAD

Lynne and I owned a cattle ranch in Arkansas, WAAAAY out in the country. We used to have neighborhood parties where entire clans would show up, everyone bringing a dish or two.

I always brought this salad and a keg of beer, which insured a very warm welcome every time. I like to think the welcome was because of my wonderful salad, but it could have been the beer.

FOR 2

1 can black-eyed peas, rinsed and drained

1 sweet red pepper diced

1 medium onion, diced

3 green onions, cut into 1-inch lengths, green part included

2 stalks celery, cut into ¼-inch slivers

¼ cup olive oil (or more to taste)

Juice of 1/2 lemon

¼ teaspoon dried oregano or dried dill

Salt and pepper to taste

Note: instead of the lemon juice, olive oil and herbs, you can use bottled Italian dressing.

Toss everything together and chill for at least an hour. Before serving let it come to room temperature.

WALDORF SALAD

This salad is a classic from the famous Waldorf-Astoria Hotel in New York. I've stayed there a few times (at the expense of one client or another) and it's quite a trip. Just sitting in the lobby and watching who comes in and out is quite a trip.

It takes just a little work but gives an air of elegance to a meal, so serve it with something special, or if you're trying to impress your guests. After you mix it all together be sure you serve it immediately.

For 4

½ cup mayo

½ cup sour cream

1 tablespoon honey

2 cups apples, cored and diced-unpeeled

1 cup celery, diced

½ cup chopped walnuts

1 cup green grapes, halved

FASTEST SALAD ON THE PLANET

This salad is courtesy of my grandmother, a world-class cook if there ever was one. Since she was from Germany I assume that's where it came from.

If it takes you more than 3 minutes to make you've had too much to drink. Don't let it sit around, just toss and serve.

For 2

½ head iceberg lettuce, torn into bite-sized pieces

2 tablespoons vinegar

3 tablespoons sugar

4 tablespoons heavy cream

Mix the sugar and vinegar until the sugar is dissolved and stir in the cream. Toss with the lettuce and serve. If you remember 2,3,4 you won't need to look at the book.

CHEF ED'S ALL-AMERICAN POTATO SALAD

Once in a great while you need to put some time in the kitchen, sort of like a heavy work-out at the fitness center. You'll also eventually need a recipe for potato salad.

I challenge anyone, professional chef or otherwise, to come up with a better tasting potato salad. It's good for a picnic, church supper, party, or just for that special someone in your life. If you don't have a special someone, this salad will help you get one.

For 4

7 medium-sized red or yellow potatoes, peeled, boiled, drained, and cut up into 1-inch pieces.

3 hardboiled eggs, peeled and coarsely chopped (after boiling, plunge them into very cold water for a few minutes and the shells will come right off)

1 medium sweet onion, diced fine

3 stalks celery, diced fine

12-ounce jar of diced pimentos

THE DRESSING

½ cup of mayo

¼ cup salad dressing

1 tablespoon white wine vinegar

½ tablespoon dry mustard

1 tablespoon sweet pickle relish plus a little juice from the jar

Salt and pepper to taste

In a small bowl, thin the mayonnaise with the vinegar. Add the mustard and sweet pickle, plus a little juice from the pickle jar. Add salt and pepper and stir it up, then taste. It should taste good to you, but strong, because potatoes are bland.

Put the potatoes in a large bowl, and break them up with a fork, leaving large and small lumps and some just sort of mashed. Add onions, celery, eggs, and pimentos. Pour the dressing over, and gently fold everything together. It should be good and moist. Now adjust to suit your taste. Serve chilled.

VEGETABLES IN SOUR CREAM SALAD

I first tasted this in a New York delicatessen and fell in love with it. You can put in any vegetables you like, sliced radishes for instance, but I think it tastes best this way. For some reason, I think it's Russian-Jewish in origin.

Serves 2

1 small cucumber, peeled, seeded, and cut into ¾-inch dice

1 small green pepper, cut into ¾-inch dice

1 small sweet onion, cut into ¾-inch dice

1 small carton sour cream

2 tablespoons dried parsley

Salt and pepper

Mix everything together in a bowl, and chill.

NOTE: For a different taste, skip the parsley, and substitute 2 tablespoons dried dill weed.

CHEF ED'S SALAD SUPREME

Everyone should have a salad that can be made into a main dish. You never know when unexpected company will show up or when you have some meat, fish or chicken leftover and want to do something with it.

However, this salad is good enough so you can forget the leftovers and do the whole thing from scratch.

For 4

1 can black beans, rinsed and drained

1 small can whole kernel corn

1 sweet red pepper, chopped

1 stalk celery, thinly sliced on the diagonal

1 can whole green beans

2-3 scallions, chopped, green parts included

2 cans whole potatoes, cut into quarters

1 cup grape tomatoes, halved

Juice of one lemon

¼ cup extra virgin olive oil

Sprinkling of dried oregano

Salt and pepper

Combine all the ingredients except the olive oil and toss thoroughly to disseminate the lemon juice. Refrigerate until ready to serve. Add the olive oil, toss and serve at room temperature.

NOTE: Now it's decision time. You can add steak cut into 1-inch pieces, cooked whole peeled shrimp, or fried chicken breasts from the deli, cut into 2-inch pieces. Just layer your choice neatly on top and serve with some crusty bread.

Fruit Salad with Chef Dugan's Dressing

This is a dressing I created because I don't care for the usual poppy seed dressing for fruit salads. I think it's the best fruit salad dressing ever, and many others have agreed with me.

Serves 4

A variety of your choice of fresh fruit in bite-sized pieces (I like watermelon, cantaloupe, apple slices, pineapple chunks, and seedless grapes).

1 package of mixed baby greens

1 8-oz carton sour cream

1⅓ tablespoons of honey

¼ cup orange juice

Place greens on a plate, and arrange fruit on top. Mix sour cream, honey, and orange juice together. Pour over salad.

NOTE: You have a lot of leeway with this dressing. You can make it sweeter by adding honey or spruce up the tartness by adding orange juice.

Mediterranean Artichoke Salad

In my last restaurant, Let's Do Lunch! this was one of our biggest sellers and, since I would not share the recipe, many caterers also bought it from us.

Try tossing it with some pasta, and it make a main dish.

Incidentally, this recipe was published in Cruising World Magazine, a great magazine for people who love living on the water.

Serves 4-6

Two 14-oz jars of artichoke hearts, drained

12-oz jar of roasted red peppers, drained

12-oz jar pitted Kalamata olives, drained

1 teaspoon dried oregano

1/3 cup very good olive oil

3 tablespoons white wine vinegar

3 tablespoons honey or to taste

Put the drained artichoke hearts in a large bowl, and add the roasted red peppers which you have cut up into large slices or pieces.

In a separate bowl combine the vinegar, honey, and oregano. Mix well and taste. It should be tart/sweet. Add more honey or vinegar until it tastes the way you like it. Pour the dressing into the vegetable mixture, stir well, and put in a storage container. Let it marinate for at least a day, stirring occasionally. Before you serve the salad, taste it once more and adjust if necessary.

SANDWICHES

PAPER-THIN GRILLED CHEESE SANDWICH

I started off the salad section with a recipe from White Trash Cooking and I'll do the same for this section. It's simplicity itself. and a side that's just begging to join it is a can of Campbell's Tomato soup. Actually, I prefer their Tomato Bisque with a little cream added, but that's up to you.

For 2

4 slices of soft white bread – like Wonder Bread. No other bread will do.

4 slices of Velveeta cheese – no other cheese will do.

Heat an iron skillet or non-stick pan with 1 or 2 generous pats of butter. Put your slices of Velveeta cheese between the two slices of bread.

Now place one sandwich in the hot pan. With a spatula, mash the sandwich flat and toast it on both sides until the cheese melts and the bread is nice and brown. Keep mashing because the flatter the sandwich the better.

Do the same with the other sandwich, heat the soup, and enjoy.

PHILLY CHEESE STEAK SANDWICH

I was born and raised in Philadelphia and I know my cheese steaks. If you're ever there, you can get original cheese steaks at **Pat's** and **Gino's.** Depending on who you talk to, either Pat or Gino invented the Philly Cheese Steak. The bonus you get from these two locations is that you're not very far from one of the most incredible Italian street markets in the US.

You're going to need the very best hoagie rolls that you can find, crusty on the outside, and a jar of Cheez Whiz. Not Velveeta, and certainly not any other kind of cheese—Cheez Whiz! Now we can begin:

Serves 2

¾ lb. good round steak in 1 piece (you can use sirloin if you like)

1 green pepper, cored and cut into long, thin slices

1 onion, halved and sliced into very thin slices

1 jar Cheez Whiz

Olive oil

2 hoagie rolls

Hot pepper flakes, it you like

It's a good idea to freeze the beef until it is rather firm, but not frozen hard. That way you can slice it, across the grain, as thin as you can get it.

In a 10–12-inch non-stick skillet, sauté the peppers and onions in olive oil until they are soft and slightly brown. Set peppers and onions aside but keep warm. At this point, you can spoon the Cheez Whiz into a microwave-safe bowl and zap it in the microwave until it's melted. Turn the heat up to high and add the beef slices. You want to fry the beef, not steam it, so keep it moving until any moisture is dissipated. Brown the beef well, and add the peppers and onions.

Cut the hoagie rolls almost in half; divide the beef mixture between them. Spoon a lot of Cheez Whiz over everything.

A GUIDE TO MAKING GREAT HAMBURGERS

Everyone knows how to make a hamburger, right? So, I'll just make a few suggestions. We all have our individual preferences about how we like our hamburgers (or cheeseburgers), but a little something different is good occasionally.

1. Use ground chuck. Fat is what gives a burger flavor. Believe me, I have had burgers made from ground sirloin, ground round, and even ground filet mignon. Chuck is better.

2. When you're making a burger, do not press down on it while it's cooking. It will lose a lot of flavor and tenderness.

3. Handle the meat as little as possible, and do not press it together. Use just enough pressure to get it to the shape you want.

4. The 21 Club in New York was as famous for its burgers, as it was for the celebrities who ate there, and the prices it charged. They put a frozen piece of herb butter in the middle of each burger to make them juicier.

5. Try putting the cheese on the bun cold. It won't

melt all over the meat, but it does give you more of a cheese taste.

6. You can take a lesson from the 21 Club and put 1-2 tablespoons of feta or blue cheese in the middle of your burger.

7. If you want to try something different, top your burger with a slice of fried green or red tomato. I prefer red.

8. Take a lesson from the BBQ restaurants and top your burger with a layer of coleslaw

.

Don't forget to stop at your friendly neighborhood supermarket and get some sides. Cole slaw, potato salad, baked beans – you get the picture. After all, you don't want to make a habit of spending TOO much time in the kitchen!

THE OKLAHOMA ONION-FRIED BURGER

History tells us this burger was created in the old frontier settlement of El Reno, Oklahoma, and has been around for well over 100 years. They still serve it today around the state, and I believe you'll find it well worth trying.

You need a griddle or cast-iron frying pan with a lot of heat under it. When the pan is smoking hot, take a ¼ pound of lean ground beef, flatten it just slightly to a burger shape, and add about the same amount of thinly sliced raw onions, placing them very carefully on top. Now flatten the whole thing out, pushing the onions into the meat with a spatula. Don't worry about what it looks like, just do as I say. As the burger is frying, press down with the spatula 3-4 times on a different section of the burger with each try. You are trying to mash the onions into the burger as it cooks. The burger should look a little rough around the edges and that's good.

Once the bottom is cooked, flip the burger, let it fry for a few minutes, and lay it on a bun, onion side up. The standard toppings are lettuce, tomato, mustard, and pickles, but you really don't need anything but the burger. No cheese please.

IOWA SKINNY SANDWICH

If you're ever driving through Iowa, Indiana, Illinois, and maybe a few other Midwestern states and see a sign for pork cutlet sandwiches, stop. If you don't, you'll miss out on an absolute culinary delight.

These sandwiches are sometimes referred to as "Skinnies," because the pork cutlets are pounded down to the thickness of a couple of quarters. I especially like them served with oven-roasted sweet potato wedges.

They're served on regular hamburger buns and, to be authentic, should extend out at least 2 inches from the sides of the bun, all around. Imagine a large salad plate between two buns and you'll get the idea.

Fortunately, there is no mystery as to how they're made, so yours can equal those of any small cafe in the Midwest.

For 2

2 pork loin cutlets

¼ cup flour

½ cup cornmeal

Salt and pepper

Dill pickle slices—these are not optional

2 cups shredded lettuce

¼ cup canola oil

Condiments (this is where you can get creative; some people put catsup, mayonnaise, or mustard on their buns, some all 3)

Put a cutlet on your cutting board and pound. You can use a mallet or hammer—whatever is handy. I use a mallet from my garage. Pound the cutlet until it is paper thin, even see-through in some spots. Make sure you keep its round shape. Repeat with the other cutlet.

On a large plate, mix together the flour and corn meal. Press the cutlets into the mixture on both sides, so they are well coated. Heat the oil in a skillet over medium heat and, when it is good and hot, fry the cutlets until they are crisp and brown. Drain on paper towels. Serve hot on the buns with whatever condiments you wish, plus lettuce and pickle slices.

NOTE: Don't use pork cutlets that the supermarket has run through their tenderizing machine—it doesn't make the same dish.

NOTE: there is another similar sandwich, on the same kind of bun, which does use those tenderized cutlets, covered with cream gravy. With them, I use Libby's canned Country Sausage Gravy. Just fry up the cutlet, put it on the bottom half of a hamburger bun, or better yet a Kaiser roll. Pour a lot of gravy on top and put on the top half of the bun. Not too gourmet but very, very good, and very, very sloppy.

<u>THE REUBEN SANDWICH</u>

Why is it called a Reuben? Legend has it that, back in the '50s, the host of *a* weekly poker game in Omaha, Nebraska, often served a grilled sandwich with corned beef, Swiss cheese and sauerkraut. His name was Reuben Kay.

There are more bad Reuben sandwiches made than good ones. Some restaurants even use corned beef round, something that should never grace your table. **If you can't find brisket, use a good deli beef sliced very thin and name it after yourself.**

You really don't need a recipe since this is just an assembly, not cooking. First, buy the best rye bread you can find, seeded if possible. You'll need about ¼ pound of corned beef, sliced very thin, for each sandwich. The other 3 ingredients are sauerkraut, Swiss cheese, and Thousand Island dressing. Spread a very thin layer of dressing on 1 slice of the bread; lay the corned beef carefully on top, followed by a slice of cheese. Put a generous layer of sauerkraut on top, add a second slice of cheese, and then some dressing. Don't skimp on the dressing. Top the sandwich with the other slice of bread.

In a skillet, large enough to hold at least 2 sandwiches, warm a couple of pats of butter until they melt. You do not want high heat, just medium low. Lay both sandwiches in the butter, cover, and cook for about 5 minutes. Take both sandwiches out of the skillet. Put more butter in, and lay the sandwiches uncooked sides down, cover, and cook for another 4-5 minutes. Serve with good kosher dills.

CREAM CHEESE AND OLIVE SANDWICH

During one of my consulting situations, I was working with the United Way of Benton, Arkansas. Our offices were a gift from a relative newcomer to the area, Jerry Van Dyke, star of the TV series **Coach**.

He had moved to Benton because it was his wife's hometown and she wanted to live closer to her family. Jerry had bought an entire block of downtown Benton and was inserting various business. One of them was an ice cream pallor and luncheonette he was setting up for his daughter. He also turned the theatre on the block into an acting studio.

We chatted just about every day, since his office was right next to mine, and knowing about my restaurant background, asked me to help him set up the luncheonette. One day, while we were doing that we stopped for lunch, and I ordered this sandwich from his cook. It was served to me with the cream cheese on bread, and the whole olives dumped on top like so many golf balls. It just goes to prove someone can screw up even the simplest of recipes. I went back in the kitchen and showed him how it should be done.

Jerry was an incredible actor and really was the star of that series. What amazed me was that he really wasn't acting that much on the show. That's exactly how he is all the time!

I also like this sandwich served open-faced on some good rye bread.

For 1

2 slices of good whole wheat or multi-grain bread

Cream cheese

Olives stuffed with pimentos, little juice also

Chop up the olives coarsely. Mix Add a teaspoon of juice from the olive jar to the cream cheese and mix thoroughly. Spread on the bread. You can make it either open-faced or not. If you really want to get fancy, trim the crusts off the bread. This is also good using bagel halves.

THE ULTIMATE TUNA SALAD SANDWICH

If you hate to cook, your inclination when it comes to tuna salad is to visit your supermarket and buy one of those pre-packaged tuna mixtures. I do it myself sometime, but never if I want to serve tuna salad sandwiches to guests.

I borrowed this recipe from the **Dean and Deluca Cookbook**. Dean and Deluca's is a landmark New York food emporium that foodies all over the United States flock to. You can also order from their online catalog. A significant amount of discretionary income is advised.

This is the best tuna salad I've ever tasted. Try it and I think you'll agree.

For 6

4 6-oz cans drained chunk white albacore tuna in water

6 tablespoons carrots, finely chopped

½ cup red onion, finely chopped

6 tablespoons fresh parsley, chopped

6 tablespoons celery, finely chopped

3 scallions, finely chopped

1 ½ cups mayo

1 small garlic clove, peeled and crushed in a mortar and pestle. If you don't know what that is, use a bowl and the back of a heavy fork.

3 tablespoons lemon juice

Salt and pepper

6 crusty rolls

Shredded lettuce

Sliced tomatoes

Put the tuna in a large bowl and mash. Add carrots, onion, parsley, celery, and scallions and mix well.

Place the mayonnaise in a small bowl and add the crushed garlic and lemon juice. Add the mayonnaise mixture to the tuna and mix well. Add salt and pepper to taste, and serve on really good rolls or bread with lettuce and tomato.

EGGS

THE WORLD'S EASIEST EGG SALAD

On one of my consulting assignments, Lynne and I used to drive from Missouri to our ranch in Arkansas, on a weekly basis. We always stopped for lunch at a little country café called Edith's. They had a wonderful buffet and our favorite item was the egg salad.

When I asked Edith for the recipe she laughed and told me just to boil some eggs and shell them, chop them up and mix with plenty of mayo – that was it!

Which proves that some of the best things in life are also the simplest.

CHEF ED'S FRITTATA

The Spanish call them tortillas, the Italians call them frittatas but they're really nothing more than an egg pancake. They make a wonderful lunch, brunch or dinner dish so give this one a try.

This is a recipe that can be altered to your liking or to what kind of filling you have available. I like it served with some catsup on the side, or a little Tabasco sprinkled on top.

For 2

4 well beaten eggs

1 can sliced or diced potatoes, drained

Package of fresh spinach

Half package of shredded cheddar cheese

2 tablespoons dried oregano

1 ripe tomato, sliced thin

I cup diced ham (optional)

3 tablespoons olive oil

Salt and pepper

To make this very simple, get all the ingredients ready for use. In the restaurant business this is called "prepping." Beat the eggs, set the drained potatoes aside, slice the tomato and measure out the rest of the ingredients.

Heat the oil, over medium heat, in a 10-12-inch non-stick skillet and spread the potatoes evenly over the bottom. Let the potatoes warm up for about 5 minutes. Carefully layer the spinach leaves over the potatoes, using about half the bag. It might look like a lot, but the spinach will shrink.

Then add the tomato slices to make an even pattern on top of the spinach and sprinkle the shredded cheese over all. If you're using ham also, this is the time to add it.

Pour the beaten eggs carefully around the edges to make sure they're evenly distributed, add the oregano, salt and pepper and cover.

Turn the heat to medium low, cover, and let the mixture cook until the eggs are firm, about 15 minutes.

HUEVOS RANCHEROS

This is your chance to show off your international cooking skills to your friends. I could give you a standard recipe for this famous dish, but why bother? This way, you can use your imagination and add sliced avocados, hot sauce, or a sprinkle of cheese over the eggs—whatever you wish.

You'll need a can of refried beans, a jar of your favorite salsa, some corn tortillas and eggs. The rest is up to you.

For each serving, you'll need 4 corn tortillas, fried in very little oil, about 30 seconds on each side, 2 eggs, fried to your liking, ½-cup heated salsa, and a generous helping of refried beans. Get it all ready while everything is warm.

Place a tortilla on each plate, spread refried beans over the tortillas, then top with the eggs and warm salsa. Serve plenty of warm tortillas on the side. I like mine buttered.

TOMATO AND CHEESE STRATA

Oh boy – a cooking lesson! A strata is a layered casserole, with similar ingredients to a quiche or frittata. (which you already know how to make) Strata's mainly consist of bread, eggs, cheese and any meat or vegetables you care to use, and are very similar to a bread pudding. To do it right, you must let the strata sit in the fridge for a few hours, or even overnight.

For 4

6 large eggs

1 pint of half and half

2 teaspoons dry mustard

8 slices of good French bread, cut into 1-inch pieces

2 cups grated cheddar cheese

2 tomatoes, sliced into ¼-inch slices

Salt and pepper

Whisk the eggs, mustard, salt and pepper, and half and half together until they are well-mixed. If you don't have a whisk just use a fork. Rub a deep casserole dish (a soufflé dish is great) with a paper towel dipped in olive oil, coating the sides and bottom.

Make 1 layer of bread on the bottom of the dish. It's okay if the bread overlaps a little, just so the bottom is well-covered. Place a layer of sliced tomatoes on the bread, and sprinkle a generous portion of cheese on top. Salt and pepper to taste.

Continue layering until the bread is used up, finishing with a layer of tomatoes and cheese. Pour the egg mixture into the casserole, cover, and refrigerate overnight, or for several hours. This is to insure the bread is well saturated with the mixture.

Let the casserole come to room temperature and then bake for 1 hour in a 325-degree oven. Brown the top slightly under the broiler, and let the dish rest for 15 minutes before serving.

NOTE: Feel free to experiment here with other ingredients. You can add diced ham, leave out the tomatoes, add a layer of cooked spinach, and change the cheese.

CHEF ED'S "TRIPLE B" COWBOY BREAKFAST

This is not only a recipe but a state of mind as well. I was watching an old Western about a cattle drive, and got to thinking of the kind of breakfast that was standard in those days. I happened to have an old tin pie pan I got from a yard sale, and I whipped up what I imagine was a typical cowboy breakfast – Bacon, Beans and Biscuits.

For 2

6 strips good, thick-sliced bacon

1 can pinto beans

4 hot buttered store-bought biscuits

2 mugs hot coffee – to be authentic it has to be black, no sugar

Tabasco sauce to taste

Sauté the bacon in a heavy skillet, preferably cast iron, until crisp. Remove and keep warm. Leave 2 tablespoons of the bacon grease in the skillet, and discard the rest.

Pour the can of pinto beans into the bacon grease, and

heat the beans, using a fork to mash some of them, and to integrate the grease.

Spoon half the beans into each tin pie plate (you can use a regular pie plate but not a dish), and add 3 bacon slices to each plate.

It's important that everything fits on 1 plate—cowboys didn't have dining room tables.

FRIED EGGS SPANISH STYLE

Here's your chance to be very continental, since this is a common recipe in the Med. Over there, it's much more of an evening meal than for breakfast, but it's your kitchen, so serve it whenever you like.

Using my fast and easy method, it won't take you very long to have this delicious meal on your table. Don't be afraid of all that olive oil, most of it will stay in the pan.

For 2

4 eggs

¼ cup olive oil

14 oz. can diced tomatoes (flavored ones if you wish)

Package of Goya fried plantains (most supermarkets will have this item)

1 package of boil-in-the-bag rice

Package of corn tortillas

First, get everything ready. Cook the rice in the bag according to instructions, open the bag and spread it out over a paper plate for later rewarming.

Do the same with the plantains (you can probably just microwave them in their package when it's time to serve) Otherwise, follow the instructions for cooking and spread them over a paper plate for later rewarming.

Place as many corn tortillas as you like on a paper plate for later rewarming.

Put the tomatoes in a small pot over medium heat.

NOTE: NOW YOU KNOW WHY I LIKE TO HAVE A GOOD SUPPLY OF PAPER PLATES HANDY.

Put the olive oil into a 10-12-inch skillet and warm over medium heat for a minute or two.

Add the eggs to the oil, being careful not to break the yolks. Cook until the edges begin to crisp up and brown nicely. At this point, you can flip them if you don't want sunny-side up eggs. While the eggs are frying, micro-wave the rice, plantains and tortillas. The tortillas only need about 45 seconds.

Divide the rice onto two plates, spoon some tomatoes over it, place the eggs and plantains alongside and serve with the warm tortillas.

DEVILED EGGS

You never know when a batch of deviled eggs will come in handy. They're a must-have for a picnic, great for appetizers, and a wonderful side with sandwiches.

The standard deviled egg filling contains hardboiled egg yolks, dry mustard, salt, pepper, and mayonnaise. But you can also add fresh or dried herbs, sweet pickle, finely chopped anchovies or sardines, finely chopped green onions, or just about anything that strikes your fancy.

I use a small spoon to fill them, and top them with a piece of pimento or some parsley to make them pretty.

Instead of mayo, you can also use salad dressing, sour cream, yogurt, or a mixture of several of them. After you've selected whichever moistener you plan to use, hard-boil the eggs and shell them. As I mentioned earlier, the eggs will shell easier if you cool them in ice water for about 5 minutes after taking them out of the hot water.

Then halve them lengthwise, remove the yolks, mash them, and add a moistener. Some obvious choices for toppings are chives, anchovies, chopped onion, and perhaps mustard.

A BASIC RECIPE FOR QUICHE

There is saying that "real men don't eat quiche" Two of my very good friends are Adrian Street and his wife Linda. Adrian was several times World Lightweight Wrestling Champion of the world, loves quiche, and I would not say that to him if I were you. As this is being written they're making a documentary of Adrian's life over in Great Britain.

This is my basic recipe that takes you to the point where you can add different treatments: seafood, meat, vegetables, or leave it plain. The Quiche Lorraine you may have heard about, contains the standard quiche mixture with the additional of bacon pieces.

I've tried quiche with every conceivable kind of cheese and decided on Laughing Cow Cheese. It's a processed Gruyere cheese that comes in little round cartons filled with foil-wrapped wedges of cheese, and can be found in just about any supermarket. I have had quiche in many, many restaurants, and they have never come close to being as good as this one. On the other hand, if you can't find Laughing Cow, just about any kind of snacking cheese will do.

For 4

1 9-inch frozen deep-dish pie shell

3 large beaten eggs, blended with enough half and half or cream to make up 1¾ cups

4 wedges of Laughing Cow Cheese, cut into ½-inch pieces (it helps to freeze it a little to make it easier to cut) If you use other cheese it's about two cups.

Salt and pepper

Pre-heat oven to 375. Prick the pie shell with a fork all around the sides and on the bottom. Bake in oven for about 10 minutes, watching carefully to see that it just browns. Remove the shell, cool it. Arrange the cheese and whatever filling you have chosen evenly over the bottom, and pour in the egg mixture. It should reach to about ¼ inch from the rim.

Suggested fillings

1 cup cooked shrimp, chopped coarsely

6 strips crisp bacon, crumbled

1 package of spinach, blanched and chopped

1 cup cooked broccoli, chopped

1 small jar pimentos

1 cup cooked asparagus, chopped

1 cup bay scallops

1 cup diced ham

2 cups sautéed mushrooms

1 cup crabmeat

NOTE: I try to err on the side of too much egg mixture rather than too little, so you may have a small amount that won't fit. Don't try to force it.

Place on the middle rack of the oven, with a plate underneath to catch any overflow, and bake for 40-45 minutes until it becomes puffed and brown. Let the quiche cool for 30 minutes before slicing it into wedges. You can test for doneness by sticking a toothpick down the center. If it comes out clean, it's done; if not, put it back in the oven a little longer.

NOTE: Quiche freezes well and, since 2 pie shells come in one package, you could make two and freeze one. Just double the recipe.

MAKING A SAUCE

THREE EASY STEPS TO SAUCE MAKING

This is a good place to give you a little advice on sauces. A nice sauce can kick the meal up a few notches. Also, think about placing the sauce on the plate first, and laying the entre on top – very elegant looking.

I'm sure you already know you can buy packaged dry sauces at your supermarket but having access to a basic white sauce will greatly expand your choices. Below are portions for thin, medium, and thick white sauces. You use a thin sauce for soups, meats, chicken, or fish; a medium sauce for pasta, casseroles, or vegetables; and a thick sauce for soufflés and dips. The following proportions make 1 cup of sauce.

When making a sauce, you must be certain to cook the flour for a minute over very low heat, or the sauce will taste like flour. I suggest you take the pan off the heat before adding a liquid to a flour-based sauce. This prevents the sauce from getting lumpy.

STEP 1: PICK YOUR SAUCE CONSISTENCY

Thin:
1 Tbs. butter
1 Tbs. flour
1 cup liquid

Medium:
2 tabs butter
2 tabs flour
1 cup liquid

Thick:
3 tabs butter
2½ tabs flour
1 cup liquid

Melt butter in a saucepan over low heat, and add flour. Stir and cook for 2 minutes. Remove from heat, and add liquid. Stir until combined, and return to heat. Cook for another 2 minutes, until it thickens.

STEP 2: PICK YOUR SAUCE LIQUID

Your choice of liquid depends on what kind of sauce you need. For example, you can use chicken broth for chicken dishes, beef broth for beef dishes, fish broth for fish dishes, and vegetable broth for just about anything.

You can also use red or white wine. If you want a deeper color to the sauce you made with beef broth, use some Kitchen Bouquet. Adding spices, such as dill weed, thyme, or parsley, or lemon or lime juice, will give these sauces a different taste. A spoonful of tomato paste will produce a lovely tomato cream sauce, and a tablespoon of curry powder will produce a curry sauce. Swirling in 2 extra tablespoons of butter, 1 at a time, will make a very rich sauce.

STEP 3: PICK YOUR HERBS, SPICES, AND FLAVORINGS

Basil
Catsup
Cayenne Pepper
Cheese
Chili Powder
Chives
Curry Powder
Dill
Dry Mustard
Horseradish
Lemon Zest or Juice
Lime Zest or Juice
Mustard
Orange Zest or Juice
Oregano
Parsley
Rosemary
Tarragon
Thyme
Tomato Paste
Tomato Relish
Tomato Sauce
Worcestershire Sauce

Keep in mind that quite often the only difference between a sauce and a soup is the presentation. For instance, you can use a pureed cream of black bean soup as a sauce over chicken breasts, for instance.

BEEF

"STUFF" ON A SHINGLE

That's the polite way to introduce a wonderfully historic dish that got its start in our armed forces. If you've never been in the service, but want to try it, just be sure you stand up and sing the Stars Spangled Banner before serving.

<u>For 2</u>

½ pound ground beef

½ pound bulk pork sausage

1 heaping teaspoon flour

1 small sweet onion, diced

1 cup, more or less, of milk

Dash of Tabasco (optional)

Combine the hamburger and sausage and fry over medium heat until well browned. Add the onion and continue cooking until the onion is soft. Add the flour, mix well, and add the milk. The mixture will thicken, but if it gets too thick, add more milk. You want it the consistency of a thick soup.

Once the dish is made, you have many options. You can serve it over toast, over a baked potato, over plain or cheese grits, English muffins, rice, or as a side with scrambled eggs. Add Tabasco if you wish.

CHEF ED'S SPECIAL BEEF STEW

This is entirely my creation. I came up with the idea since the traditional beef stew recipes quite often gave you either over-cooked vegetables, tough beef, or both. This stew will produce tender-crisp vegetables and succulent beef.

Although you can do the entire thing from scratch, to keep the promise of this book, I've put in a lot of short-cuts. Trust me, it will still be very delicious. However, be forewarned, it will also be a trifle expensive. If you try to save money on the beef you'll ruin the recipe, so if you're tempted to do so, please go out and buy a can of Dinty Moore's Beef Stew and leave mine alone.

For 4

1 lb. NY Strip, Rib-Eye or Filet Mignon, cut into 2-inch thick pieces (I prefer the Filet Mignon)

2 medium carrots, peeled and cut into 1-inch slices (or you can use a can of carrots)

1 sweet onion, halved and cut into ½ inch slices

2 celery stalks, cut into ½ inch slices

2 cans diced potatoes

1 can or jar beef gravy

1 can beef broth

1 small can of tomato sauce

½ cup red or white wine (optional)

3 tablespoons Worcestershire sauce

1 tablespoon dried thyme

1 tablespoon dried parsley

Put the canned beef broth into a pot and add the celery and onions. Cook over medium high heat until the celery and onions are crisp-tender, about 15 minutes. Add the spices and the can or jar of beef gravy, the Worcestershire sauce, and tomato sauce. Turn the heat to very low. If using, add the wine now.

Turn the heat up to medium, and when the mixture begins to simmer, cook for another 10 minutes., then add the beef pieces. Continue to cook for 3 more minutes and serve.

IRISH POT ROAST

The first time I saw this recipe in an Irish cookbook, I thought there must be a misprint. I'd always believed that pot roasts had to be braised in broth or wine. Not necessarily. This makes an incredible pot roast, and when it's finished, you have lots of natural juices with which to make gravy. The flavor of the meat and gravy will be outstanding.

For 4-6

3–4 lbs. pot roast with a little fat on it (I prefer chuck)

1 can beef stock

Salt and freshly ground pepper

1 tablespoon thyme

3 tablespoons flour

If you want to use one of those throw-away pans you get at the supermarket it's okay, but be sure you cover the roast tightly with foil. Otherwise, use a heavy roasting pan with a lid.

First, you need to cut a little fat off the roast and render it in a skillet or in the heavy roasting pan. Then brown the roast on all sides and discard the fat.

Sprinkle the roast with thyme (the Irish sometimes rub it with grainy mustard). Cover tightly (use foil if you bought a throw-away) and cook for 2½-3 hours at 250 degrees. The secret is in long, slow roasting at a low temperature.

Remove the roast, bring the pan to the top of the stove, add flour, and brown slightly. Remove from heat and stir in broth. Return to heat and cook until gravy thickens.

It may sound a little unusual but the Irish like to serve this over elbow macaroni.

FRENCH POACHED BEEF TENDERLOIN

Just because you hate to cook doesn't mean you're poor – right? That's good, because we're dealing with some expensive meat here.

The French have made this for years and know what they're doing. You're talking about several pounds of very expensive beef, and the recipe is only for 4 people, so invite guests that you really like, or your boss.

The technique translated is tenderloin on a string, or *"a la ficelle."* The concept is easy: you tie up the meat with a string and suspend it from the sides of the pot into broth and vegetables. The tenderloin must not touch the bottom of the pot, thus the string.

It's poached briefly in the broth and served rare to medium-rare. I don't know how you can get beef any more succulent than what this recipe provides, and the flavor is remarkable.

Note: Instead of beef broth you can use other liquids such as vegetable broth, maybe add a little wine or beer, whatever comes to mind.

For 4-6

2-3 lbs. beef tenderloin in a uniform piece, tied, with 2 ends of string left loose

5 cans beef broth

¼ cup olive oil

2 cups water

1 large garlic clove, quartered

6-8 small red potatoes, peeled and cut into quarters

2 carrots, peeled, cut into 3-inch julienne

2 stalks celery, cut into 3-inch julienne

1 medium onion, halved and sliced thinly

½ teaspoon dried thyme

NOTE: You can add turnips, rutabaga or winter squash if you wish. The more vegetables the better!

In a heavy, deep saucepan with two handles, add the oil and sauté the cut-up vegetables over medium heat for about 5 minutes. Add the beef broth and the water, and simmer the vegetables for about 20 minutes until they are tender but still a little crisp. You can let the mixture rest off the heat.

NOTE: If you don't have a saucepan with 2 handles, tie the string to a long spoon in 2 places and suspend over the liquid. Make sure the string is long enough.

About 15 minutes before you are ready to serve, reheat the vegetables to a simmer, tie the tenderloin to both handles and submerge in the hot liquid, being careful not to let the meat touch the bottom of the pot. Poach the tenderloin for about 15 minutes. Lift the meat out of the broth, and let rest for 10 minutes. With a slotted spoon remove the vegetables to a platter.

Slice the meat across into 4 pieces, place some of the vegetables around each serving, and pass some store-bought Creamy Horseradish Sauce if you wish.

SWISS STEAK

The name is misleading because it has nothing to do with the Swiss. It comes from the British term "swissing," meaning to smooth and flatten meat before cooking. The British call it stewed steak although it really isn't a stew.

This is a typical braise so long, slow cooking is involved. It can be done on top of the stove or in the oven. I prefer braising in the oven, to better control the outcome, but it can be done either way. Remember, braising requires just 2-3 cups of liquid, otherwise you have a stew.

For 4

2 lbs. sirloin or round steak, at least 1-inch thick, trimmed of fat (save the fat)

Flour as needed

1 tablespoon olive oil

1 onion, finely chopped

1 carrot, finely chopped

1 sweet pepper, chopped

1 stalk celery, finely chopped

1 garlic clove, finely chopped

1 can diced tomatoes

1 can beef broth

1 small can tomato sauce

½ cup red wine

1 tablespoon dried thyme

1 tablespoon dried rosemary

Use a meat tenderizer or the edge of a saucer, and pound the steak until it is about half its original thickness. Take the heel of your hand and press as much flour into the meat as it will hold.

Put the saved fat scraps, along with the olive oil in a heavy, oven-proof casserole; over medium heat, render as much fat as you can from the scraps. Discard them, and add the meat. You can cut the meat into serving pieces first, if you wish. Brown the meat slowly, about 15 minutes on each side, and set aside.

Add the onion, carrot, celery, garlic, and the herbs to the pan; stir and cook for 1 minute. Add the beef broth, tomato sauce, wine, and diced tomatoes; stir well and return the meat to the pan.

When the sauce begins to bubble slightly, cover the casserole tightly and put in a 250-degree oven. Roast 2½ hours or more. (NOTE: If you choose to do this on the top of the stove, keep the dish to a slow simmer.)

You can either thicken the sauce with a flour and beef broth mixture, or leave it slightly thinner. If you want to thicken it, reserve about a ¼ cup of the beef broth to mix with the flour.

Serve the meat with the sauce and creamy mashed potatoes.

COUNTRY FRIED & CHICKEN FRIED STEAK

Here's a perfect example of two different ways to treat the same cut of beef. For Chicken Fried Steak, the steak is first battered, then almost always deep fried. The batter puts a semi-hard crust on the steak. It's served with gravy that has some cream or evaporated milk in it.

To make a simple batter, break an egg into a bowl and whip it a little with a fork. Add about a ½ cup of flour and the same amount of mile. You want the consistency of a thick soup. Dip the steak into the batter, let the excess drip off and immerse it in about 2-inches of very hot oil. Cook for about 3 minutes, turn it over, do the same, and serve. There, you just made chicken-fried steak just like the pros.

For Country Fried Steak the steak is browned, and then brown gravy is made. During the old days on the trail, the gravy consisted of some evaporated milk, some leftover coffee and a little water, using flour as a thickener.

The truth is, once the steak is pounded to about a ¼-inch thickness and some flour is rubbed into it, you can do almost anything you want with it. You already have the recipe for Chicken Fried Steak and now here's the recipe for Country Fried Steak. The idea is to tenderize the steak and then fry it. If you don't have a meat tenderizer, you can use the edge of a saucer, just like the pioneers did.

Whichever way you make the steaks, they fit right in with buttermilk, cornbread, greens, and mashed potatoes.

NOTE: It's okay to cheat a little if you want to buy some packaged gravy. They sell both the brown and white kind at most supermarkets.

<u>**Serves 2**</u>

1 lb. round steak, top or bottom (feel free to use sirloin)

4 tablespoons peanut oil (or lard)

4 tablespoons flour plus ¼ cup

½ cup cream

1 cup beef broth
Salt and pepper (a generous amount of freshly ground pepper)

All the cookbooks I have read tell you to use a metal meat tenderizer or the edge of a saucer to pound the flour into the meat. It works, but you end up with a floury mess. My method is to use the saucer or tenderizer to make both sides of the surface of the meat very rough and indented. Then, using the heel of your hand, press as much flour as you can into the ridges. Do this to both sides. Put a layer of flour on a plate and lay the steak on top. Then sprinkle another layer of flour on top of the steak, and set aside for 15 minutes. No mess.

This dish really calls for an iron skillet with a heavy lid. If you don't have one, you should.

Put 3 tablespoons of oil in the skillet, and heat until it's almost smoking, using a medium-hot setting. Cut the meat into 2 individual steaks, and brown thoroughly on both sides; turn the heat down to moderate, cover, and simmer for about 10 minutes. Remove the steaks, and place in a warm 200-degree oven.

Add enough oil to the skillet to equal about 3 tablespoons. Add the 4 tablespoons of flour and stir, making sure you get the brown bits on the bottom. When the flour begins to brown just a little, remove the pan from the heat, add the beef broth, and mix well. Return to heat and stir until it thickens. Add the cream and a good amount of pepper, and cook for another 3 minutes. Serve the steak smothered in gravy.

CARPETBAG STEAK

A carpetbagger was a Northerner who move to the South after the Civil war to loot and plunder. Why there's a steak named after them I'll never know.

This is a very old recipe that seems to have passed out of existence, so I'm reviving it. Try grilling one of these guys if you want to impress your guests.

Get a 2-inch thick steak, a New York Strip, a Sirloin or a tri-tip. Cut a pocket almost all the way through the middle and stuff it with oysters.

Secure the open end with toothpicks and grill it over hot coals for about 10 minutes on each side. Remember you want the oysters to cook also. Put a large pat of butter on top, let it rest for a few minutes, and slice it across the grain. Another version calls for the steak to be stuffed with fried oysters, but take care not to overcook them.

STEAK AU POIVRE

I was first introduced to this dish by Art Buchwald, the late Washington Post syndicated columnist and humorist. Art was also a Pulitzer Prize winner and, for many years, wrote a column from Paris for the New York Herald Tribune.

When he returned from Paris, we met for dinner and he suggested I try this dish. When it turned out too spicy for my taste, he reached across the table, speared it and put in on his plate. He told me he was counting on that happening when he suggested it. You can make it as spicy as you wish.

This is a chance to impress someone with the cooking skills you probably don't have. Just knowing about this recipe is impressive enough. A baked potato and a tossed salad is all this meal needs.

For 2

2 New York Strips, 1½-inches thick

2 tablespoons black peppercorns, coarsely crushed (use a plastic bag and hammer)

2 tablespoons olive oil, divided use

4 tablespoons butter, divided use

¼ cup brandy

½ cup red wine

Using 1 tablespoon of the olive oil, thoroughly coat the steaks on both sides. Sprinkle ½ tablespoon of pepper on 1 side of a steak, and press in firmly with your hands. Repeat on the second side.

Heat 1 tablespoon olive oil and 2 tablespoons butter in a heavy skillet, and sauté the steaks over medium-high heat, turning once, until they are done to your liking (2 minutes on each side will give you a rare steak). Keep the steaks warm in a 200-degree oven while you are making the sauce.

Over medium-high heat, warm the pan for 1 minute and pour in the brandy. Ignite with a kitchen match, and shake the pan until the flames cease. Add the wine and, 1 tablespoon at a time, swirl in the remaining butter. Remove the sauce from the heat immediately, pour over the steaks. and serve at once.

QUICK AND EASY FAJITAS

If this recipe were any easier, you really couldn't call it cooking. Although it uses beef, it can also be made with pork or chicken.

If you feel guilty about how little effort it takes, open a can of refried beans and make my Combination Salad to go with the fajitas.

For 4

1 ½ lbs. beef, around 1-inch thick (I like sirloin)

1 12-oz jar of salsa of your choice

2 tablespoons oil

10-inch flour tortillas

Cut the beef into ½-inch or smaller cubes. Heat the oil in a large skillet until it is almost smoking, and brown the beef, about 5 minutes. Pour on the salsa and mix well. Reduce heat to medium-low, and cook for 45 minutes, stirring every so often. You just want it to simmer slowly. The longer it simmers the better it gets.

While the mixture is cooking, heat the tortillas, wrap in foil, and keep warm in a 250-degree oven.

When the beef has absorbed most of the moisture, and the salsa is just a glaze, take a tortilla, spoon 3-4 tablespoons of the meat mixture down the center, fold in the ends, and roll it up.

CORNED BEEF AND CABBAGE DINNER

Some people will tell you that this really isn't an Irish dish. Just so you know, the Irish have been corning beef since the 11th Century! In New England, they call it a New England boiled dinner. It's easy to make, and doesn't really require a recipe, but I want to give you a few guidelines.

A lot of people cook the corned beef and vegetables together, usually adding the vegetables for the last hour. You can do this if you wish, but the vegetables will pick up a lot of taste from the heavily seasoned broth. I prefer to cook the vegetables by themselves in some boiling, salted water, thus preserving their natural taste.

Never buy corned beef round, only brisket. The round has very little fat and therefore much less flavor. Buy the largest piece you can find. Corned beef shrinks when cooking, and you want some left over for sandwiches. Although the cooking time for corned beef is long, about 3 hours, you can overcook it, so test it after 2½ hours for tenderness. If you boil corned beef rather than keeping it at a low simmer, it will get tough. Just follow the directions on the package.

After the corned beef is done, remove it from the pot, and let it cool. You will find that it appears to be in 2 pieces. Between these pieces is some unwanted fat you should cut out, as well as trimming some of the covering fat on top. However, to be good, corned beef needs a little fat.

As for your choice of vegetables, the usual is carrots, celery, turnips, onions, potatoes, and cabbage. Cut the cabbage into wedges, and tie them with a string across the middle to keep them from falling apart. Leave some root end on the onions for the same reason. Some people serve beets on the side. Rather than cook the vegetables in the beef broth, you can get a much fresher taste by cooking them in canned chicken broth separately, and then add them just before serving.

It is very important that you remember to <u>cut the corned beef across</u> <u>the grain into thin slices.</u>

PICADILLO

This dish is common around the Caribbean, each island having its own special twists. A simple sale or some fruit goes well with it. Lynne and I lived full-time aboard our sailboat and spent many happy days in the islands. This recipe brings back old memories.

For 2

2 cups cooked rice

1 lb. lean ground beef

2 tablespoons olive oil

14-oz. can crushed tomatoes or diced tomatoes

¼ cup raisins (or more)

¼ cup green olives with pimentos, sliced in half

2 tablespoons capers

1 medium onion, chopped

bay leaf

2 tablespoons parsley

1 clove garlic, minced

¼ cup white wine

1 packaged salad of your choice

Crusty rolls or warm corn tortillas

Heat olive oil in a heavy skillet, over moderate heat, and brown beef. Add onions and garlic and cook until onions are soft. Add olives, capers, salt and pepper to taste and one tablespoon of juice from the olive jar. Cook for 3 minutes and add tomatoes, wine and raisins. Cover and simmer for 10 minutes. Spoon the picadillo over rice, toss the salad and serve bread or tortillas with the meal.

CHEF ED'S MEATLOAF AND/OR STUFFED PEPPERS

I always make a meatloaf with two purposes in mind: a meatloaf meal and meatloaf sandwiches. I pay special attention to the two "t's," taste and texture. This recipe is a little different from most, since I like to load my meatloaf with a lot of veggies.

My overall goal is to make a meatloaf that's close to a pate. I like it very dense, so it slices nice for sandwiches. Hence the number of eggs and the amount of bread crumbs.

Finally, this recipe uses only beef, but you can add ground pork and/or veal if you wish.

NOTE: I like a free-form meatloaf which I shape with my hands, but you can use a loaf pan. If you use a pan, use the kind that self-drains the meatloaf, so the juices don't drown out the loaf.

For 4-6

2 lbs. ground beef chuck

1 large onion, chopped coarsely

2 stalks of celery, chopped coarsely

1 large carrot, chopped coarsely

1 large or 3 baby sweet red peppers, chopped coarsely

3 garlic cloves, minced

1 cup chili sauce

1 teaspoon dried rosemary

1 cup Panko bread crumbs

3 eggs, beaten Salt and Pepper

¼ cup heavy cream: optional (You can use cream, or broth, the idea is to make sure the meat mixture is just a little moist before you put it in the oven; it may not need anything.)

Using your hands, mix together the meats, onion, carrots, garlic, ½ cup ketchup, rosemary, thyme, salt, pepper, and Worcestershire sauce. When thoroughly mixed, add the egg, bread, and cream, and continue mixing.

Form the mixture into a firm evenly shaped loaf, either round or oblong, and place in a shallow baking dish. Spread the remaining ½ cup of ketchup evenly over the top. Bake in a 325-degree oven for 2 hours. Let the loaf rest for about 30 minutes before serving.

STUFFED PEPPERS

Using the above meatloaf recipe, skip the bread, and add 2 cups of cooked rice, cut the top off green, yellow, or red peppers, and stuff them. Put them in a pan with about an inch of water, and bake for 1 hour, 15 minutes.

LIVER AND ONIONS

A lot of folks don't like liver, even some who have never tasted it. That's beyond stupid! If you've tried it and it's just not to your taste, fine, but at least be able to say you're had it.

This is a recipe that has been pirated many times from the world-famous Harry's Bar in Venice, Italy. The only difference between this meal and Harry's is about $100.

Incidentally, most of the time liver should be cooked from rare to medium-rare. However, here, you can forget that and get the pieces nice and crispy. You can use pork, beef, or calf's liver, but I search out veal liver because I think it's the best.

For 2

¾ lb. veal or calf's liver

1 large sweet onion, halved and sliced very thin

2 tablespoons olive oil

2 tablespoons butter

Place liver in the freezer until almost frozen hard. With a sharp knife slice it into the thinnest strips you can, and about 2-3 inches in length. Set aside.

Heat butter and olive oil in a 10-inch skillet, add onions, and sauté slowly, stirring frequently until the onions are very brown and almost caramelized, about 20 minutes. Remove from skillet, and set aside.

Add a little more olive oil to skillet, turn heat to medium-high, and sauté liver until brown and slightly crispy. Add onions to pan, stir, and serve.

A conventional pairing would be polenta and a salad with vinaigrette dressing. Believe it or not, my grandmother, who helped raise me and was an incredible cook, served this with mashed potatoes and baked beans. Give it a try.

<u>*PORK*</u>

MONTE'S HAM

This recipe is named after Monte Mathews, an advertising copywriter, author, and chef. When he first arrived in New York he was given two pieces of advice: if you go to a party and wear a very expensive watch, you can wear anything else you want; and if you're entertaining a lot of people, buy the cheapest ham you can find and glaze the hell out of it.

Here's the recipe for the ham – the watch is up to you.

15 lbs. smoked ham on the bone—the cheaper the better

The Glaze:

1½ cups orange marmalade

1 cup Dijon mustard

1½ cups firmly packed brown sugar

1 rounded tablespoon whole cloves

Trim the outer skin and excess fat from the ham. Making crosshatch incisions, score the ham all over with a sharp knife. Roast in a large roasting pan for 2 hours at 300 degrees. Remove ham from oven, and increase heat to 350 degrees.

Combine all glaze ingredients, except cloves, in a bowl,

and mix well. Stud ham with the cloves, and brush entire surface of ham generously with the glaze. Return ham to oven and cook for 1½ hours, brushing with the glaze every 30 minutes. Remove from oven, brush with any remaining glaze, and allow to rest for 30 minutes.

Put several loaves of good bread on the table, a variety of mustards, and let your guests cut themselves some ham. Some good store-bought potato salad and coleslaw, and that's all you need.

WHAT TO DO WITH ALL THIS LEFTOVER HAM?

If you're single, or just a couple, dealing with a leftover baked ham can be a problem. Not to worry, I have several suggestions for you.

- First, get a sharp knife and cut all the ham off the bone. Try to get as many slices as you can and then go for the chunks.

- Next, divide the ham into single or double servings and place them in plastic wrap for later freezing. Before putting the ham in the freezer, put all the packets in a large zip lock bag. Now you have a few future meals.

Now we have the ham, what do we do with it? Here are my suggestions:

- Ham sandwiches, of course. Plain, grilled with cheese, layered with a fried egg.

- Make ham salad. Dice some ham very finely along with diced celery, onion and mix with mayo and just a touch of mustard. Make sandwiches or serve as a luncheon salad.

- Use the bone to make bean soup. Put the bone in a large pot, add some dried beans, onion and chopped sweet pepper, cover and cook on low heat for about 3 hours. This is very similar to the famous US Senate bean soup, so pretend you're a Senator and screw up the country while you're eating the soup.

- Dice some ham and add it to scrambled cheese eggs or to a quiche. I already told you how to make a quiche.

- Gently fry some ham slices and serve with eggs and potatoes.

- Add the ham to a white cream sauce (packaged is fine) and spoon over store-bought biscuit.

- Add the ham to the preceding white cream sauce, toss with some canned diced potatoes and mix with shredded cheddar cheese. Top the casserole with more cheese and bake for 30 minutes at 375 degrees.

That should give you some ideas. One thing for sure, your average cost per meal will do a nose dive and your time in the kitchen will be cut considerably.

LAST MEAL PORK CHOPS

I call these Last Meal Pork Chops because the meal is rich – make that VERY rich! If you're going to embark on yet another diet, this meal will leave you with fond memories of what real food is like.

Unless, of course, you are using my book Help – I Gotta Lose Weight! In that case you don't have to worry eating this meal – with my weight loss method, you can eat it and still lose weight. Check it out on Amazon.

This recipe is about as down-home as you can get and is so easy you'll hardly know you were in the kitchen. And delicious doesn't even begin to describe it.

For 4

4 1-inch thick pork chops, bone in

2 large sweet onions, cut in half and sliced very thin

1 cup heavy cream

Salt and pepper

Trim off a few slivers of fat from the pork chops, leaving the rest on. In a 15-inch skillet, over high heat, render the slivers of fat, remove them, and then add the pork chops. Brown them on both sides.

Smother the chops with the onions, add salt and

pepper, and cover the skillet securely. Turn the heat down very low, and cook for 2½ hours. DO NOT PEEK!

After the time has elapsed, uncover the chops, and remove them to a warm oven.

Add the cream to the onions and liquid in the pan, raise the heat, and boil until the mixture is reduced to a sauce-like consistency.

NOTE: The meal isn't complete without having some creamy mashed potatoes and greens (collard or mustard greens sprinkled with pepper sauce), or some spinach sautéed in olive oil and a little balsamic vinegar. Season the onion sauce with salt and pepper, and spoon over the chops and potatoes.

FIREHOUSE PORK CHOP CASSEROLE

A very simple dish that is always well received. It truly is a firehouse veteran, so you know that timing isn't too important, since you never know when the fire-bell will ring.

What you are doing here is building several layers of food, starting with the chops, then the onion, then thick-sliced potatoes, then lima beans, finally adding some beef broth, salt, and pepper.

For 2

2 thick-cut bone-in pork chops

2 medium russet potatoes, peeled and thickly sliced (about ⅓ inch)

1 can lima beans (or green beans if you prefer)

1 can beef broth

1 large sweet onion, sliced thin

Salt and freshly ground pepper

Peel the potatoes, slice them thick (at least 1/4 inch), and put aside in a bowl of water so they don't turn brown.

Peel the onions, cut them in half (any way you want), and slice them thin. Set aside.

Open the can of lima beans and drain.

The pork chops should have a layer of fat around part of them; slice this off, and put the fat in a skillet. Turn the heat to medium, and cook for about 10 minutes, or until the fat pieces are brown and crisp, and have given up their fat. Discard the pieces.

Turn the heat up slightly, place the chops in the skillet, and brown them on both sides. Layer the onion slices over the chops, then the potatoes, and finally spread the lima beans over all. Pour enough beef broth over the mixture to a depth of about ¾-inch. Salt and pepper to taste, and cover. Turn the heat to low, and simmer for 1 hour or more.

BAVARIAN PORK & SAUERKRAUT

What makes this dish special is an old German way of cooking sauerkraut. It really does make a difference. As far as most Germans are concerned, you can't overcook sauerkraut – the longer the better. There is an especially good brand of sauerkraut imported from Germany and made with white wine. It comes in jars shaped like little barrels.

For 2

1 lb. of any cut of pork (regular or country spareribs, pork steaks, pork chops, or better yet, pork hocks)

1 can or jar of sauerkraut

1 can beef broth

2 tablespoons butter

1 small onion, chopped

1 tablespoon caraway seeds (optional)

Lightly rinse the sauerkraut in a colander, being careful not to rinse away too much of the brine (I like it better not rinsed at all). Heat butter in a large 10-inch skillet and, when it is melted, mix with the kraut. Turn heat low, cover, and cook gently for 30 minutes, stirring kraut every so often (German cooks do this as a matter of course, and it makes a world of difference in the final product).

Sprinkle caraway seeds, if using, over the kraut, and then layer on the onions. Place pork over the kraut, and add half the can of beef broth. Cover again, and simmer over low heat for at least 1 hour. Add more broth as needed. It's almost a requirement that you serve mashed potatoes or spaetzle.

Spaetzle: These are sometimes referred to as Swabian Noodles and they are very easy to make. Just beat an egg in a small bowl, add 1 cup milk 1 cup flour. Mix well and add some salt and pepper.

You want a dough just a little thicker than a pancake batter, so play around with proportions. Set a pot of salted water boiling and turn the heat down to simmer. With a large spoon, dip up some of the batter and with a wet knife, clip little pieces off the end of the spoon. Don't worry about the size of the pieces but try to keep them uniform. When they're done they'll float to the top. Drain well and either butter them and serve, or sauté them in butter until they turn slightly brown.

STUFFED SPARERIBS

Grilling isn't the only way to make delicious spareribs, as this recipe will show you.

NOTE: It's perfectly acceptable to use a packaged dry stuffing such as Pepperidge Farm. If you do, substitute the water with chicken or beef broth and add sautéed chopped celery and onions.

Serves 4

2 racks spare ribs (not baby backs)

8 cups bread stuffing of your choice

Either use a cookie sheet or heavy-duty aluminum foil to cover the middle rack of your oven. Place the stuffing on the foil, molding it to the approximate size of the rib rack, and cover it with the ribs. If you're making both racks, you can "sandwich" the stuffing between the 2 racks and bake them that way. Put them on the bare oven rack and place a drip pan underneath. Otherwise, the bottom ribs will get stewed in the juices. Roast at 325 degrees for 1½ hours, or until they're crisp.

THE PLANET'S BEST BBQ RIBS

I'll admit, I'm not much of an expert on the grill, but I do love good barbecued ribs. It's more than just how the ribs taste, it's all about the great sides as well. Cole slaw, potato salad, beans and anything else that appeals to you.

As a chef, I want you to know HERE is the best recipe on the planet and I believe I got the idea from *Bon Appetite Magazine*.

Choose baby back ribs or just plain spareribs, and then follow these three simple steps: First you season the ribs, then you bake them, and finally you grill them.

For 4

4 lbs. baby back (4 racks) or St. Louis-Style spareribs (2 racks)

2 tablespoons kosher salt

1 tablespoon dry mustard

1 tablespoon paprika

½ teaspoon cayenne pepper (optional)

½ teaspoon ground black pepper

1 cup BBQ sauce (I like Kraft Thick 'N Spicy)

Preheat oven to 350 degrees and combine the salt, dry mustard, paprika, cayenne pepper, and black pepper in a small bowl.

Place each rack on a double layer of foil, and sprinkle the rub all over the ribs. Wrap the foil around the racks, and place on a baking sheet. Bake the ribs until they are very tender but not falling apart, so check the baby backs after 2 hours and the spareribs after 3 hours. Unwrap the ribs carefully, and pour any residual juice into a small cup and reserve. When the ribs have cooled completely, rewrap and set aside.

NOTE: At this point you can refrigerate them for up to 3 days until the final step. They get firmer and develop much more taste if you wait at least a couple of days before you finish them off.

For the final step, build a medium-hot fire in either a charcoal or a gas grill. Add enough chicken broth or water to the reserved juices to make 1½ cups, and whisk in the BBQ sauce to blend. Grill the ribs, basting with the sauce and turning frequently, until lacquered and charred in places and heated through – about 10 minutes. Transfer to a cutting board, cut the ribs into serving pieces and pass additional sauce. **WOW!**

LAMB

FRENCH LEG OF LAMB

If you're going to serve lamb to company, this is the dish you want.

The English call it Spoon Leg of Lamb because when it's done, the meat is so tender you can really eat it with a spoon.

This meal makes an elegant presentation if you have some special guests you want to impress. Yes, it takes a little effort but in this case, it's well worth it.

NOTE: Be prepared – the lamb cooks for as much as 7 hours, so plan on that.

For 4-6

5-6 lbs. boned leg of lamb

3 medium sized onions, each stuck with 2 cloves

3 carrots split lengthwise

6 cloves garlic

½ cup olive oil

1 teaspoon dried thyme

1 tablespoon dried parsley

1 bay leaf

2 cans diced tomatoes

1 cup red wine

Salt and pepper

1 can white beans

Rub the lamb with salt and pepper, and arrange on a rack in a roasting pan. Surround with the onions, carrots, and 3 garlic cloves. Pour the olive oil over the bones and vegetables, and roast in a 400-degree oven for 30 minutes, reduce heat to 350 degrees, and continue roasting for 30 more minutes. Remove from heat, and reduce heat to 200 degrees.

Transfer the lamb to a large casserole, and add the remaining 3 garlic cloves, 1 teaspoon each of salt and pepper, thyme, bay leaf, parsley, tomatoes, and vegetables from the roasting pan. Rinse the roasting pan with the red wine, and pour over the lamb.

Cover the casserole, as well as the cover, tightly with heavy duty foil. You want to make it as airtight as possible. Return to oven, and bake for 6 hours.

Transfer the lamb to a platter. Discard the bay leaf,

and skim any excess fat from the pan juices. Remove the cloves from the onions and discard.

Puree all the vegetables in a blender and add to the pan juices. Stir in the parsley.

Slice the meat and serve with the sauce spooned on top.

Canned white beans and a nice salad go well with this meal. Also, be sure you have a jar of mint jelly on the table – it's an incredible addition to any lamb dish.

GRILLED BUTTERFLIED LEG OF LAMB

Any supermarket meat department can butterfly the lamb for you. If you feel ambitious, buy an already boned leg, take off the netting that holds it together, spread it out and get a sharp knife.

At this point you should remove as much fell as possible. Fell is that shiny transparent layer you see on some parts of the leg. Carefully slide a point of a knife under it and slice up. When it begins to tear, you can pull most of it off. This is not something you need to worry about—get as much as you can and forget about it.

Spread the leg out so that it is open and flat. There will be thin spots and thick spots. Keeping in mind that you want to keep the lamb in 1 piece, make some vertical slices in the middle of the thick spots, so that as much meat is exposed as possible. You will still have thick pieces as well as those that are not so thick. When it is finished, some of the meat will be rare, some medium rare, and some crispy.

Rub the meat generously with olive oil, and spice it anyway you wish. Slivers of garlic stuck in the meat are one of the best ways. Oregano is always nice.

Get the grill good and hot, and lay the meat, cut side

down, about 6 inches from the coals or flames. Cover, and grill for about 10 minutes. Do not allow it to char. Flip the meat over, cover, and grill for another 10 minutes.

Check the thickest part with your meat thermometer, and when it registers whatever degree of doneness you want, remove it from the grill, and let it rest. Its best medium rare.

Carve in diagonal slices across the grain. It's okay to flip it a few times while grilling to make sure you get it nice and brown on both sides.

POULTRY

THE VERY BEST WAY TO ROAST A CHICKEN

Before I say anything else about chicken you should know about brining. Brining is an age-old technique that adds moisture and enhances taste. The optimum soaking time is 4 hours, but even a shorter time will make a flavorful difference.

The brine solution is usually a mixture of sugar and water. Make sure everything is well dissolved before placing the chicken in it. You can also add brown sugar or wine. Now, on to the main subject.

A lot of cookbooks will tell you to roast the chicken on a rack, and they explain how to properly truss it, and ask you to roast it at any number of temperatures. I've done all that, and have a better and much easier way to do it.

First, remove the little bundles of fat from near the tail. You don't use a rack and you don't truss the bird. What you do is roast it at 500 degrees, moving it around every so often to prevent it from sticking to the bottom of the roasting pan. Check from time to time with your thermometer until it reads 175 degrees, take the chicken out, and let it rest for at least 20 minutes.

<u>NOTE: If you don't own a cooking thermometer go out and buy one. They are indispensable to helping you get</u>

food to the right temperature without burning it.

If you want a lovely brown chicken, before you roast it, cover it all over with a thick coating of soft butter. Don't bother to baste. These instructions apply whether the bird is stuffed or not. Incidentally, the back of the oven is hotter than the front so that's where you want to stick the chicken's feet. You know, sort of putting its feet to the fire.

QUICK AND EASY FRIED CHICKEN & CREAMED GRAVY

Somewhere along the way I concluded that I just didn't want to invest the money in a deep fryer, since I rarely used one. I also didn't want to miss out on that wonderful cream gravy that my favorite down-home restaurant offered with their fried chicken. Culinary expert that I am, I came up with a wonderful solution and here it is.

Most supermarket deli operations, as well as KFC and other well-known fried chicken chains, offer pretty good fried chicken. Some of it's very good. So, go out and buy a bucket, or a basket or whatever amount you need.

Next, take the pieces of chicken and pick or rub off some of the fried batter, taking only the crispy parts but no skin. You almost can't have too much, but a 1/2 cup should be sufficient for 2 people.

Take a small skillet, add 3-4 tablespoons of butter and a dash of olive oil, and slowly melt the butter over medium heat. Add the batter pieces, and sauté for a few minutes. Then add several tablespoons of flour and cook for a few minutes.

Add a ¼ cup of canned chicken broth and a ½ cup of milk, cream, half and half or evaporated milk, whatever strikes your fancy. When the gravy thickens, add some salt and **LOTS** of freshly ground pepper. Adjust the gravy with more milk until it gets to a nice consistency. You won't believe how good that gravy is – creamy, flecked with cracklings, and spicy with pepper!

Mix up a big batch of mashed potatoes, not forgetting my trick of adding a few tablespoons of mayo to make them nice and creamy. Crisp up the chicken in a 450-degree oven, and serve. Heat a can of collard or turnip greens if you want to take an imaginary trip to the South.

KING RANCH CHICKEN

Legend has it that this dish originated on the famous King Ranch in Texas. If you want to serve four to six people on the cheap, this is the way to go. It's also relatively fast and very easy.

For 4-6

4 skinned and boned chicken breast halves

2 tablespoons butter

1 tablespoon safflower oil

1 green bell pepper, chopped

1 medium onion, chopped

2 (10-ounce) cans Rotel diced tomatoes with chilies

1 can cream of mushroom soup

1 can cream of chicken soup

12 (6-inch) corn tortillas, cut into quarters

8 oz. shredded cheddar cheese

1 can chicken broth

1 cup water

Put the chicken breasts in a saucepan with the broth and water. Heat to simmer, turn heat low, and poach for 20 minutes. Remove chicken and coarsely chop or shred.

Melt butter and oil in a large skillet over medium heat. Add bell pepper and onion, and cook until slightly soft but not brown. Remove to a large bowl, and thoroughly mix the chicken, onions, peppers, diced tomatoes, both cans of soup, the broth, and the water.

Arrange one third of the tortilla quarters on the bottom of a 13 x 9 x 2 greased baking dish. (I use a round dish, so the tortilla quarters make a nice pattern.) Top the tortillas with one third of the chicken mixture, and sprinkle evenly with 2/3 cup of cheese. Repeat layers twice, reserving 2/3 cup of cheese. Cover the top loosely with foil.

Bake at 325 degrees for 35 minutes, remove foil, and sprinkle with remaining cheese. Bake another 5 minutes. Let stand for 10 minutes before serving.

All you need is a nice tossed salad to round out the meal.

NOTE: Don't be concerned about how the divided chicken mixture works out. If you have a lot left for the top layer or just a little, it really doesn't matter.

This dish is somewhat like a thick stew, and once you serve it, everything will blend in together. The cowboys were not interested in presentation. Serve it with some warm tortillas on the side.

BREADED LEMON CHICKEN BREASTS

A simple recipe but very good. Sometimes I think that if it weren't for lemons, the number of chicken recipes in the world would be cut in half.

For 2

2 skinned and boneless chicken breasts

Juice 1 lemon

1 clove garlic, peeled and crushed

1 egg, beaten with 3 tablespoons of water

1 cup flour

1 cup dried bread crumbs (try Panko)

1 tablespoon olive oil

2 tablespoons butter

Place chicken breasts, smooth side up, in shallow dish, pour lemon juice over, add garlic clove broken into several pieces, and cover tightly with plastic wrap. After 2 hours turn chicken, cover, and marinate for 1 more hour.

Place egg in shallow bowl, flour in another, and bread crumbs in another. Dip chicken breast in egg wash, then in flour, back in egg wash, and finally into bread crumbs. Press bread crumbs firmly into chicken, and place on clean plate. Repeat with another breast. Refrigerate for 1 hour.

Warm butter and olive oil in sauté pan over moderate heat. Place chicken breasts in pan, and sauté gently for 15 minutes. Turn breasts, and repeat for 15 minutes. Be careful not to have the heat too high or the coating will turn too dark before the chicken is done. Squeeze a little lemon juice on top of the breasts, and serve.

This dish is good with just about any side – mac and cheese, baked potato, pasta and tomato sauce, whatever's handy.

ROAST CHICKEN WITH GARLIC

This dish has been around for ages and is usually called "Chicken with 40 Cloves of Garlic." You really don't need that much garlic but that's the name of the dish. If you don't like a lot of garlic move on.

Here's the drill. When the chicken is ready to serve, you squeeze a garlic clove onto a piece of crispy French bread, spread it around like butter, and dip it in the sauce. You'll think you're in "garlic heaven."

For 4

16 good-sized cloves of garlic, unpeeled

1 whole frying chicken

6 tablespoons olive oil

1 teaspoon dried tarragon

Salt and pepper

Rub the olive oil all over the chicken, until it is well coated. Sprinkle the tarragon all over the top of the chicken.

Place chicken in a deep pot and pour any remaining olive oil into the bottom. Place the garlic cloves all around the chicken, between the legs and body, and putting a few inside the cavity. Add salt and pepper. Cover the pot tightly with foil, and place a lid over the foil. The chicken must be sealed as tight as you can manage.

Place in a pre-heated 275-degree oven for 1½ hours. Remove chicken from the pot, let it rest for about 10 minutes and carve to your liking. Pass the garlic cloves around with the French bread.

This dish is rich so keep the side dishes simple; a tomato and cucumber salad is good. The leftover chicken can be served cold with a nice vinaigrette sauce.

CHICKEN ENCHILADAS OR BURRITOS

Whether you crave enchiladas or burritos, this is a wonderful way to use up leftover chicken from any of the preceding recipes.

If you don't have any leftover chicken, just buy a package of skinless, boneless chicken breasts and poach them in lemon water for about 20 minutes.

I've tried to make this as quick and easy as I can so the prep time is cut to a minimum. We have two stages of preparation: first, the filling and second the cheese sauce.

Basically, both are wraps of either corn or flour tortillas. What makes this dish special are the tomatillos (Mexican tomatoes).

For 2-4

Stage One:

3 cups leftover chicken shredded, or 2 small skinless and boneless chicken breasts, poached and shredded

3 tablespoons cooking oil

1 small onion, chopped

1 sweet red pepper, chopped

1 clove garlic, chopped (optional)

2 tomatillos, chopped

2 tablespoons salsa (red or green)

1 tablespoon dry cumin

1 tablespoon dried cilantro flakes

<u>Stage Two:</u>

6 medium-sized flour tortillas (or corn tortillas)

1 jar of Mexican cheese (you may need two)

1 small can diced green chilies

Heat the oil in a skillet over medium heat. Add onion and sauté until soft, about 3 minutes. Add red pepper and garlic, and continue cooking for 3 minutes. Add tomatillos and cook until they soften, about 5 minutes. Add chicken, cumin, cilantro, and the salsa, stir well and set aside.

Melt the Mexican cheese and stir in the diced green chilies. Lightly cover the bottom of a shallow casserole with several spoonful's of the cheese sauce.

Lay out 6 tortillas and spoon about 4-5 tablespoons of

chicken mixture along the center of each tortilla, leaving about 1 inch on each end. Fold each side of tortilla over the chicken mixture, making a tube. Place the tortilla in the casserole, seam side down. Continue with the rest of the tortillas. Spoon the remaining cheese sauce over the tortillas, making sure they are completely covered. Sprinkle a little paprika over the dish if you like.

Bake 30 minutes at 350 degrees. This meal is good with rice or refried beans.

GRILLED TANDOORI CHICKEN WITH INDIAN SALAD

I know, you hate to cook and want to spend as little time in the kitchen as possible. That's why I wrote this book.

However, there are some occasions when you need to go to a little trouble to impress some special guests, or just one special guest. This recipe will fill the bill.

If you like Indian food, this is a fun dish to make over the weekend. If you have never tried Indian food, this recipe is a good introduction. I've never been to an Indian restaurant that didn't have their version of Tandoori Chicken. In India, the chicken is cooked in a clay grill called a tandoor, which is how it gets its name.

For 2-4

8 chicken drumsticks, skin removed

1 large carton of plain yogurt

1 tablespoon red chili powder

1 tablespoon coriander powder

2 cloves garlic, minced

1 tablespoon dried ginger

1 tablespoon Garam Masala powder (you can find this in the spice section of any supermarket)

1 tablespoon salt

Red food coloring

1 stick butter

1 sweet onion, halved and cut into ¼-inch slices

Lemon juice to taste

Prick the chicken with a fork all over, about 10 times for each drumstick.

In a wide, deep bowl, large enough to hold all the chicken pieces, add the yogurt and 1 cup of water. Add the next 6 ingredients and mix well. Add 2 teaspoons red food coloring, and stir until you have a beautiful red mixture. If you like it more colorful, add more coloring, it won't hurt anything.

Stir in the chicken, making sure every piece is totally covered. Cover, and marinate for about 6 hours or overnight. The longer you marinate, the better it will be.

Heat up a charcoal grill until the coals are gray and

very hot. Melt the butter. Remove the chicken from the marinade, and let most of it drip off. With a basting brush apply the melted butter all over the chicken, and grill as you normally would, until the chicken is done to your satisfaction.

Halve the onion, and cut crosswise into ¼-inch slices. Toss the onion slices with salt and lemon juice, and serve with the chicken.

Here's the perfect side dish for Tandoori Chicken:

1 cucumber, seeded and finely diced

1 carton plain yogurt

1 large tomato, seeded and diced

½ small, sweet onion, minced

1 ½ tablespoons fresh lemon juice

¼ teaspoon ground cumin

1 tablespoon fresh mint, chopped (dried is okay)

Salt

Mix everything together, chill and serve. A package of Rice Pilaf would also go well.

CHEEZ-IT CHICKEN

I'll bet you only thought of Cheez-It's as a snack. This recipe gives you another use for them. It's delicious, fun and easy to make.

For 2-4

Get some boneless, skinless chicken breasts and a box of Cheez-Its. Cut the breasts into strips as thick as your little finger, and toss them in a bowl with some mayo.

Take about 2-3 cups of the Cheez-Its, put them in a freezer or storage bag and, using a mallet, or a meat tenderizer, or even a hammer, pound them until they are fine crumbs. Put the chicken strips in the bag and toss until they are well coated.

Sauté the strips in a mixture of half butter, half olive oil until they are nicely browned and crisp.

I also suggest you mix half mayo and half ketchup in a dipping bowl, and dip the pieces in it. Yum!

ROASTED CHICKEN & VEGETABLES

This is pure comfort food. It's easy to prepare, and I suggest you do more vegetables than you normally would. They make a wonderful hash with the leftover chicken.

For 4

3–4 lb. frying chicken

4-5 medium red potatoes, unpeeled

3 large carrots, peeled and cut into chunks

1 medium acorn squash, peeled and cut into chunks

3 medium yellow squash, cut into chunks

2 red sweet peppers, cut into eighths

2 medium onions, peeled and quartered

2 large cloves of garlic, chopped

10–12 cherry tomatoes or 1 cup grape tomatoes
4 tablespoons dried rosemary

3 tablespoons olive oil

NOTE: If you like a little crisper skin on your chicken put it uncovered on a plate in the refrigerator overnight.

Place chicken in a roasting pan (not on a rack) and surround it with all the vegetables, except the tomatoes. Drizzle the olive oil over the chicken and vegetables, and sprinkle the rosemary over all.

Place in a 375-degree oven and bake for 1½ hours. From time to time, stir the vegetables around in the pan drippings. Add the cherry tomatoes to the dish during the last 20 minutes of cooking.

Remove chicken from roasting pan, and carve into serving pieces. Place on a platter, and surround with vegetables. Spoon pan juices over all, and serve.

You've got to have plenty of crisp rolls or bread to sop up the juices with this meal, as well as a simple salad.

Chicken Hash from the remains: Cut up the leftover chicken and vegetables into bite-sized pieces. Mix everything together well, and add salt and pepper. Put 2 tablespoons of olive oil in a skillet over medium heat, and add the chicken and vegetable mixture. Press down with a spatula and sauté for about 10 minutes. Flip the mixture over, brown on other side, and serve. I like scrambled eggs or a green salad with this.

FISH & SHELLFISH

SHRIMP CREOLE

We've all heard about this dish, and there must be hundreds of recipes for it, but this one from the late Paul Prudhomme is one of the best. He was the king of Cajun and Creole cooking and the culinary world will miss him.

As with all authentic Cajun dishes, it contains the "Cajun Trinity," celery, onions and green peppers.

Serves 4

1 lb. shrimp, peeled and de-veined

1 cup bottled clam juice

1 cup onions, chopped

½ cup celery, chopped

¾ cup green pepper, chopped

1 large clove garlic, chopped

1 bay leaf
½ tablespoon dried thyme

1 tablespoon dried basil

1 can diced tomatoes

1 small can tomato sauce

1 teaspoon sugar

1 tablespoon olive oil

2 tablespoons butter

Salt and pepper

4 cups cooked rice-in-the-bag (two bags)

In a 10-inch sauté pan, heat olive oil and butter until butter is melted. Add the onions, and cook until brown, about 5 to 7 minutes. Add celery, pepper, garlic, and bay leaf, and sauté for 5 to 7 minutes. Add half of the clam juice, and cook down for 10 minutes. Add spices, tomatoes, rest of clam juice, and cook for 10 additional minutes. Add tomato sauce and sugar, turn heat to low, and cook for 15 minutes. Just before serving add shrimp, and cook until pink.

I like to serve this in a wide soup bowl. Take a custard cup, spray it with cooking spray, and pack it with hot rice. Invert the cup in the middle of the soup bowl and tap gently so the rice comes out. Spoon the Shrimp Creole all around the rice, and sprinkle the entire dish with parsley. Welcome to the French Quarter!

SHRIMP AND GRITS

When Henry Flagler was heading to Key West building his railroad, he had a lot of workmen to feed every day, and Henry didn't get to be as rich as he was by being a spendthrift.

Grits were cheap (they still are), and fish and shrimp were close by and free for the taking. I'm sure this dish was served a lot. There are many ways to make it, but this one, from **Charleston Receipts** (no, I didn't misspell the name), published by the Junior League of Charleston in 1950, is my favorite.

For 2

1½ cups small raw shrimp, peeled

2 tablespoons onion, chopped

2 tablespoons green pepper, chopped

1 teaspoon Worcestershire sauce

1 tablespoon tomato catsup

1½ tablespoons flour

1 cup of water, or more

Salt and pepper

3 tablespoons safflower oil or bacon grease

4 hot hardboiled eggs

Tabasco sauce

Make grits according to package, and cover. Keep warm.

Fry onion and green pepper in fat, over medium heat. Add flour, and cook until it is well mixed with the vegetables.

Remove skillet from heat, add water, and stir. Return skillet to heat, and cook until sauce thickens. Add Worcestershire sauce, catsup, and shrimp. Simmer for 4 minutes, until the shrimp are just done.

Shell eggs, cut in half, and place 2 eggs on each plate. Sprinkle with Tabasco.

Spoon grits onto plate, and serve shrimp alongside.

NOTE: The gravy will mix with the grits and that's the way it's supposed to be. Biscuits are good with this meal also.

SHELLFISH DUMP

This dish can be made with shrimp, lobster, crawfish, blue crabs, or king crab legs, or a mixture of some of them. Traditionally it's served on a bed of newspapers, so to clean it up, you just need to roll up the paper and discard.

Also, the seafood is usually served with the shell on so a certain amount of picking is required, which is half the fun.

For 2-4

3 lbs. of the shellfish of your choice

8 small red potatoes, unpeeled

4 ears corn on the cob

1 lb. store-bought coleslaw

1 jar prepared seafood cocktail sauce

1 package shrimp-boil seasoning

2 sticks clarified butter

Lots of leftover newspaper

Bring a large kettle of water to the boil, pour in the seasoning, and simmer for 15 minutes. Meanwhile, prepare another large kettle with boiling water, and add the potatoes and corn. Cook for 30 minutes.

After 15 minutes, add the shellfish to the seasoned water, and turn off the heat. Let it sit for another 15 minutes. Get the condiments ready. Cover the entire kitchen or dining table with 3 to 4 layers of newspaper. Drain the shellfish and vegetables from the kettles, and dump in the middle of the table.

When I say dump, that doesn't mean you can't have paper plates full of coleslaw, boiled red potatoes, and corn on the cob placed around the table. You will also need a bowl of melted butter flavored with lemon juice, and 1 of seafood sauce.

I usually just fill a bowl full of Chili Sauce and add horseradish and lemon juice to it. You also might want a bowl of Ranch Dressing as an additional dip. This is a casual meal, so relax and forget your table manners! If you want to take it to the extreme, try it with 4-5 Maine lobsters or Florida lobster tails.

FISH FILETS WITH LEMON-BUTTER AND CAPER SAUCE

You can use any firm fleshed fish filet like catfish, snapper, grouper, mahi mahi, tilapia, or salmon. One nice thing about this recipe, it gets you in and out of the kitchen in record time.

For 2

2 fish filets

3 tablespoons butter

1 tablespoon olive oil

4 tablespoons capers, drained

¼ cup flour

1 large lemon

Make sure your lemon is quartered and your capers drained before you start the fish. You might be tempted to skip the capers, which is alright, but they do add a little dash of flavor to the dish.

Spread the flour on a large plate and dip the fish filets into it, coating both sides.

Over moderate heat, warm the butter and oil in a

skillet, and sauté the filets for about 3 to 4 minutes on each side. They should be a golden brown. Set aside on 2 paper plates.

Quickly turn up the heat, squeeze 2 quarters of the lemon into the pan, and add the capers. Pour this sauce over the filets, and serve with the remaining lemon quarter.

A good side is a package of Stouffer's Macaroni and Cheese and some store-bought coleslaw.

NOTE: You can use the cooked fish filets stuffed into some hard taco shells, add some salsa, lettuce and tomato and you have a fish taco. Team it with some refried beans.

POACHED FISH FILETS WITH TOMATOES

A very simple meal that Lynne and I eat often. It's the combination of flavors and textures that we like best. I especially like codfish for this dish but I've also had good luck with Chilean Sea Bass. That last fish can be very expensive so check out the price first. Thicker filets are better than thin ones.

For 2

1 can stewed tomatoes (use diced if you prefer)

¼ cup dry white wine

1-pound cod filets

2 medium potatoes

Heat the stewed tomatoes, add the wine and simmer for about 10 minutes. Add the cod, and simmer gently for about 10 more minutes. Or you can poach the cod in lemon flavored water, and add just before serving. What you are trying to do is not overcook the cod.

This dish is wonderful with my special mashed potatoes. This recipe is also included in the Vegetable Section but, since we're here, I might as well include it.

The way I make them is, after they're cooked and

drained, put in plenty of butter, milk or half and half, and 2 heaping tablespoons of mayonnaise. Mash or whip them with a beater until they're smooth. The mayo makes them very creamy and, with this meal, they're great with the stewed tomatoes spooned over them.

CHEF ED'S CRAB CAKES

While growing up in Philadelphia, I remember being taken to the corner tavern on Friday nights for crab cakes, French fries, and coleslaw. To show you how long ago that was, beer distributors delivered cases of beer to your home, just like the milkman.

I was too young to drink, but I still remember the damp, beery smell of the tavern. Over the years, I have tried everyone else's recipe for crab cakes, but still like mine best. Anyone in Baltimore will tell you to only use fresh blue crab, not the kind that is pasteurized. But for those of us who live elsewhere, the only suggestion I have is use only lump crabmeat, even if it's canned.

For 2

½ lb. crab meat (lump crabmeat only)

3 tablespoons mayonnaise

½ teaspoon celery seed

½ teaspoon dry mustard

½ teaspoon Worcestershire sauce

½ teaspoon Old Bay Seasoning

¼ cup green pepper, minced

2 scallions, minced, white part only

1 tablespoon celery, minced

1 small jar diced pimentos, drained

2 slices of good stale bread, cut into ½-inch cubes

Squeeze of fresh lemon juice

1 egg white, beaten lightly

1 cup dried bread crumbs

2 tablespoons butter

2 tablespoons olive oil

Soak the bread in ¼ cup of milk until soft. Drain, and squeeze excess moisture out. In a bowl gently mix together all ingredients, except dried bread crumbs, being careful not to break up the crabmeat too much. Spread half of the dried bread crumbs on a plate. Shape the mixture into 4 small cakes, and place on plate. Sprinkle some more dried crumbs on top, and gently press into cakes. Fry in the butter and olive oil for about 4 minutes on each side.

SCALLOPS POACHED IN WHITE WINE

Once the scallops are poached, there are several ways to treat them. You can have them simply poached and sautéed in butter, but you should try other ways to serve these delectable morsels. Please note that Sea Scallops are large, and Bay Scallops are much smaller.

Try tossing them in a pasta salad or sautéed in lemon butter. I really don't think poaching is the best way to treat the smaller bay scallops, unless you are very careful with your timing. Scallops can get tough fast.

For 2

1 lb. sea scallops

1 tablespoon scallions, minced

1 bay leaf

1 teaspoon salt

1 cup dry white wine

½ cup water

Heat the water, wine, scallions, bay leaf, and salt in a small skillet, and simmer for 10 minutes. Add the scallops. The liquid should cover the scallops. If not, add some more water, and return to the simmer. Remove from heat immediately, and let the scallops cool to room temperature in the liquid. When cool, strain the liquid, and save for a sauce if you like.

NOTE: you can serve the scallops cold in a pasta or rice salad, make a sauce with the poaching liquid, a small can of tomato sauce and cream. Simmer the sauce for a few minutes, add some lemon juice and serve over the scallops.

RICE, DUMPLINGS & PASTA

RICE TORTILLAS

NOTE: Almost of the time I make a rice dish I use Boil in a Bag Rice.

A Spanish dish that's a great way to use leftover rice. Serve them hot with just about anything your imagination can come up with. The recipe serves four for a snack or two for a meal.

One way to serve them is with a variety of salsas brought to room temperature. They're also wonderful as a side to almost any main dish.

For 2

1 cup cooked rice

1 medium potato, peeled and grated

2 scallions, sliced thin, green part included

½ small onion, minced

1 garlic clove, minced

2 tablespoons fresh parsley, chopped

3 large eggs, beaten

2 tablespoons paprika

3 tablespoons olive oil, divided

Salt and pepper

Heat 1 tablespoon olive oil in a non-stick skillet over medium-high heat. Add the rice, potato, onions, and garlic, and stir-fry for about 2 minutes, or until the mixture begins to color.

Spoon the mixture into a large bowl, and stir in the eggs, paprika, and parsley. Add quite a lot of freshly ground pepper and salt, or the dish will be too bland.

Clean the skillet, and heat the remaining oil over medium heat. Using a 1/3 cup measure, spoon the mixture into the pan, allowing some space for the tortillas to spread. Fry for 2 to 3 minutes on each side, until they are a beautiful golden brown. Drain on paper towels, and keep warm in a 200-degree oven until the entire batch is done.

COMPANY RICE

This is a wonderful dish to serve when you're having company. Julia Child is due the credit for this recipe. More than her recipes, I think she deserves credit for opening an entirely new world of cooking to the American public. What would we have done without her?

It takes a little prep time, and it's hard to make in small amounts, but it's a spectacular main course for a small dinner party. Once it's assembled, you can relax with your guests.

For 4-6

4 cups cooked rice

Extra virgin olive oil, as needed

Freshly squeezed lemon juice

Salt and freshly ground pepper

1 cup fresh parsley, chopped

1 red pepper, diced

3 scallions, sliced, including green parts

½ cup pine nuts, sautéed in olive oil

6 fresh basil leaves, sliced thin

1 cucumber, seeded, salted, and drained

¾ cup diced feta cheese

2 cups broccoli florets, blanched to crisp-tender

½ cup pimento stuffed olives, sliced in half

3 tablespoons capers, drained

2 cups grape or cherry tomatoes, sliced in half

2 lbs. cooked shrimp, shelled and de-veined

Mayonnaise to be passed separately

NOTE: You can also use lobster, crab, scallops, chicken, pork, whatever you wish. I like shellfish with this dish.

Toss the rice in a bowl with a little olive oil, lemon juice, salt, pepper, and the parsley. Taste and correct seasonings. This is important because the flavor of the rice will set the standard for the rest of the dish. You want it not too oily and a little tart.

Add the red pepper, scallions, basil leaves, cucumber, and shrimp, and toss gently until it is well-mixed.

Arrange the rice on a serving platter, on a bed of greens if you wish. Decorate the platter by arranging the broccoli florets around the edge, and sprinkling the green olives, capers, pine nuts, tomatoes, and the feta cheese over all to make a pretty presentation. A final touch could be quartered hardboiled eggs. Cover with plastic wrap and refrigerate until serving time.

Serve with a small bowl of mayonnaise and invite the diners to stir it into the rice mixture, or you can give each one a small bowl with mayo in it.

LOW COUNTRY RICE

At one time, rice helped make Charleston, South Carolina, a very wealthy city. If you grow it, you tend to eat it, and eat it they did.

This recipe is sometimes called Red Rice, and although it makes a "gracious plenty" as they say in the South, you can't make too much. Besides, it freezes very well.

It makes a wonderful side for many dishes such as fried chicken or ham, or boiled shrimp.

For 4

1 bag of cooked Boil-in-the Bag rice

1 medium onion, chopped

1 stalk celery, chopped

1 green pepper, chopped

1 28-oz can diced tomatoes

4 strips bacon, fried crisp, and grease reserved

Add onions, celery, and pepper to bacon grease, and sauté over medium heat until soft, about 10 minutes. Add rice to skillet and mix thoroughly with vegetables. Cook for about 5 minutes, stirring so rice doesn't stick to pan. Add diced tomatoes with their juice. If the mixture looks too dry just add a little water to it.

Just before serving, crumble bacon on top.

RED BEANS & RICE

A famous Louisiana dish that I'm sure you've heard about. You can add some sliced Boudin sausage if you want, and some folks like to add a smoked ham hock.

It's very similar to the preceding recipe for Low Country Rice, so you might want to leave out the tomatoes and just add the beans.

For 2

1 can red kidney beans

1 small onion, minced

1 jalapeño pepper, seeded and diced

1 cup chicken broth

1½ cups cooked rice

2 strips bacon, cut into ¼-inch dice

Tabasco sauce to taste

Salt and pepper

Heat a small saucepan over moderate heat, and add the diced bacon. Cook until the bacon is a little crisp, about 5 minutes. Add the onions and pepper, and sauté for 5 more minutes. Add the beans and their liquid to the pot with the chicken broth. Cook over low heat for 10 minutes. Salt and pepper to taste.

Mound the rice in a shallow soup bowl, and surround it with the bean mixture. Sprinkle with Tabasco.

HOPPIN' JOHN

Although there are many versions of how this dish got its name, but its roots lie in Africa and the West Indies. For some reason, it's become a tradition to serve it on New Year's Eve and is supposed to bring good luck.

Don't leave out the ham hocks though.

For 2

1 bag of Rice in a Bag, cooked

1 can chicken broth

1 small onion, chopped fine

2 smoked ham hocks

1 can black-eyed peas

2 teaspoons canola oil

2 tablespoons dried parsley

Tabasco or hot pepper vinegar to taste

Heat the oil in a small saucepan, and sauté the onions until they are soft and slightly browned. Add the chicken broth, the black-eyed peas and the ham hocks and parsley. Cook over low heat for about 30 minutes.

Cut the meat off the ham hocks into bite-sized pieces, and mix back into the peas. Put a big helping of rice on a plate, and top with the pea mixture. If the rice has cooled just lay it out on a plate a microwave it for 30 seconds.

GOOD LUCK!!!

NOTE: You can use this as a side dish, or if you want to go really country, serve it as the main course with cornbread, buttermilk, and the Combination Salad in the Salad Section.

DUMPLINGS

ABOUT DUMPLINGS

In my award-winning cookbook, *Help-I Gotta Cook!* (Cookbook of the Year) I have some recipes for dumplings, but given the tone of this book, if you're in the mood for dumplings just go to the supermarket and buy a package of gnocchi or other dumpling.

Back in the Pork Section, I give you a recipe for Spaetzle, which is a dumpling, just in case you want to make some from scratch.

PASTA

SAUCING & OTHER PASTA SUGGESTIONS

I disagree with the pasta rule that says pasta is best when served al dente. I don't like pasta that's only three-fourths cooked, and I have never been able to tell the difference between the taste of well-cooked pasta and pasta served al dente. However, that's your decision.

Pasta should be cooked in large amounts of boiling, salted water. Sometimes it needs to be rinsed after cooking. If you're making macaroni salad, for instance, rinse it 3 to 4 times under the faucet, drain it thoroughly, and toss it with a little olive oil. Then, when you mix in mayonnaise or salad dressing, it won't turn into a sticky mass after it cools.

To stimulate your imagination, I've listed the basic sauces and some suggestions about how to incorporate them into your pasta dishes.

The 5 basic sauces are tomato, pesto (basil, olive oil, and garlic), butter and cream, Alfredo, and olive oil. Additionally, there are many sauces made with clams, and they are covered in the Sauce Section.

Tomato Sauce: There are millions of people who adore

garlic, and others who can't stand it. This is a garlic-free sauce and you can add as much as you like, or not.

Put 1 can of Fire Roasted Diced Tomatoes into a blender, and add a small can of tomato sauce, 2/3 cup of red wine, 2 chopped sweet mini-peppers, a teaspoon of sugar, and 1/3 cup olive oil. For seasonings, I use either a tablespoon of Italian Seasoning or the same of Oregano. Mix it all together for about a minute, and then cook it over medium heat for 10 minutes. If you want a smoother sauce, use a food processor.

When this sauce is finished, fry up a little ground beef until it still has a little pink in it and add it to the tomato sauce. That will give you Bolognese Meat Sauce.

Pesto: Pesto is almost a necessary ingredient in flavoring Italian vegetable-based soups. If you want to make your own, put 2 tightly packed cups of fresh basil leaves, 2 tablespoons of pine nuts, 2 chopped cloves of garlic, ½ cup olive oil, and ½ cup good Parmesan or Romano cheese into a blender, and blend well. Pesto also freezes well. Or you can buy jars of some pretty good pesto at most supermarkets.

Butter and Cream: Heavy cream is called for here. It's best to heat the cream, add a lot of butter, and then grated Parmesan or Romano cheese. You can make it as rich as you want, but please don't try this with nonfat or 2% milk. This is the sauce you use for Fettuccine Alfredo, but I have a dietetic version under that listing in the Pasta Section.

Alfredo: Just buy a jar at your local supermarket.

Olive Oil: It's not a bad idea to toss your pasta with a little bit of olive oil or butter before adding anything else. It helps separate the strands or pieces, and adds a little flavor.

Suggestions for additions to your pasta dishes:

- Shrimp
- Clams
- Scallops
- Lobster
- Mussels
- Pork or beef
- Italian sausage
- Chicken breasts
- Meatballs
- Meat sauce
- Green beans
- Broccoli
- Cauliflower
- Green peas
- Zucchini
- Yellow squash
- Sautéed green or red peppers
- Sautéed eggplant
- Asparagus

FETTUCCINE WITH SHRIMP & VEGETABLES

If you're short of time check this one out. It should take twenty minutes from start to finish and you'll have a delicious dish to serve. Some nice crusty break and a tossed salad will round out the meal.

For 2

1 small zucchini

1 small yellow squash

3 Roma tomatoes, diced

½ lb. shrimp, shelled cooked and de-veined (just buy them this way in the supermarket)

1 lemon

4 tablespoons olive oil

Lots of grated Parmesan cheese

Salt and pepper

½ lb. fettuccine

Cut zucchini and yellow squash into ¼-inch slices. Blanch in salted boiling water for 1 minute. Drain and set aside. Place shrimp in a small bowl and toss with a little lemon juice.

Boil fettuccine until done and drain. Return to pot, add olive oil and other ingredients and toss well. Add salt, pepper, some lemon juice, Parmesan cheese and serve.

SPAGHETTI CASSEROLE

This is the first dish my wife Lynne served when she invited me over to her apartment. The second time, she served a Tuna Casserole, and ever since, I've cooked every meal for the past 44 years.

However, this book would not be complete without this recipe. It really is delicious and very easy to make. Just toss a salad and the meal's finished.

For 2

1 lb. ground chuck

½ cup onion, chopped

¼ cup green pepper, chopped

1 can cream of mushroom soup

1 can tomato soup

1 can water

1 clove garlic, minced

½ lb. spaghetti, cooked and drained

½ cup shredded cheddar

2 tablespoons cooking oil

Brown chuck, onion, garlic, and pepper in a skillet for 10 minutes, stirring frequently. Add soups and water. Stir thoroughly. Mix in spaghetti, and pour into an oven-proof casserole dish. Top with cheese, and bake at 350 degrees for 30 minutes.

NOODLE PUDDING (KUGEL)

Even people who hate to cook should have one or two culinary surprises in their repertoire. This recipe is from the old country, as Europe used to be called, and I got it from my grandmother. I believe it's origins are both German and Jewish.

This dish seems to go exceptionally well with pork.

For 2-4

2 cups dried eggs noodles (I like wide but medium is okay)

3 tablespoons unsalted butter

2 large eggs, lightly beaten

1 cup regular cottage cheese (not low-fat)

½ cup regular sour cream (not low-fat)

½ cup raisins, pre-softened in water or white wine

1 sweet apple, cored, and cut into ¼-inch dice

¼ cup dried apricots, cut into ¼-inch dice
½ teaspoon salt

¼ teaspoon ground cinnamon combined with ¾

teaspoon sugar

Cook noodles in a large saucepan of boiling salted water until tender. Drain well in a colander, and toss with butter in a large bowl.

While noodles are cooking, whisk together the eggs, cottage cheese, apples, raisins, apricots, sour cream, salt, and pepper. Stir into noodles.

Butter a deep 1-quart casserole or baking dish, and add noodle mixture. Sprinkle the top with cinnamon sugar. Bake at 375 degrees for 1 hour. If you want a dish that's less on the sweet side, skip the cinnamon sugar.

NOTE: Before you put the dish in the oven, make sure it's a little bit moist. Baking and the absorption of the pasta will take up a lot of the moisture. You don't want it too dry, so add a little milk if you feel the need to. It should be a little on the "soupy" side.

EASY LASAGNA

Lasagna dates to Roman times so you might expect a lot of variations. Bolognese lasagna uses only spinach pasta, in Liguria they use pesto, Neapolitans layer the sheets with tomato sauce and mozzarella, and Calabrian's prefer ricotta. This is delicious, easy and just a regular, all-American way to make lasagna.

For the meat sauce, you use your favorite spaghetti sauce mixed with the ground beef. You can also use ground chicken or turkey if you prefer.

For 4

2 tabs extra virgin olive oil

1 package lasagna noodles

1 jar spaghetti sauce

1 jar Alfredo sauce

1 Lb. ground beef

Container of Parmesan cheese

Fry the beef in a skillet over medium heat until it is brown. Pour in the pasta sauce, mix well, and set aside. Cook the lasagna noodles according to directions and drain.

Line the bottom of your lasagna pan with a layer of

pasta, trimming it with a sharp knife or scissors so it fits evenly. Spread a layer of your meat mixture, and sprinkle lightly with some Parmesan cheese. Add another layer of pasta, and spread with about 1 cup of the Alfredo sauce. Repeat until you have 3 layers of meat sauce and 2 layers of Alfredo sauce, ending with the meat sauce. Bake for 30 minutes until it is slightly browned on top. Let it rest for 10 minutes, and serve.

MACARONI AND CHEESE

Macaroni and cheese is nothing more than cooked macaroni, or other pasta of your choice, mixed with a cheese sauce, and baked for a while.

As often as I've made it from scratch, I really can't beat the taste and texture of Stouffer's Macaroni and Cheese. As a variation I sometimes defrost it, mix it with a ½ can have diced tomatoes, and maybe throw in some chopped chicken breasts. After that I bake it for 20 minutes at 350 degrees, and serve.

If you have something as delicious as Stouffer's at your disposal, why try to re-invent the wheel?

SPAGHETTI WITH FRESH TOMATO SAUCE

This dish is simplicity itself, quite delicious, and healthy to boot. You can add other vegetables, such as sautéed broccoli, asparagus, or even pre-cooked shrimp, but this is the way I first made it, and it got me hooked. The key to this dish is the quality of the tomatoes. If you can't find home grown tomatoes, use grape tomatoes.

For 2

½ lb. spaghetti (regular, thin, angel hair)

2 ripe tomatoes, cored, diced, and drained

4 tablespoons black olive slices or Kalamata olives, sliced thin

¼ lb. fresh mozzarella, cut into small dice

4 tablespoons extra virgin olive oil

6–8 fresh basil leaves, torn in small pieces

Salt and pepper

Make the spaghetti, drain, and toss with the olive oil. Add the vegetables, cheese, basil, olives, salt, and pepper, and toss some more. Serve with a green salad and some crusty bread. Don't you feel healthy? I also use this basic recipe, and add shrimp or sautéed chicken breasts.

VEGETABLES

BUBBLE AND SQUEAK

Even Queen Elizabeth would recognize this dish. It's very English, and I make it whenever I have leftover potatoes and cabbage. I even make it when I don't.

This is a natural partner with pork chops or ham.

For 2

2 cups cooked potatoes, cut into large uneven pieces

3 tablespoons cooking oil (lard is traditional and bacon fat will also do)

1 small onion, minced

1 cup cooked cabbage, chopped

Put half of the oil into a skillet, and sauté the onions for about 5 minutes over moderate heat. Mix the potatoes and cabbage together, add to the skillet, and toss with the onions. Add the rest of the oil.

Press down to flatten the mixture, and cook for about 10 minutes, until it begins to brown. Flip the mixture over, and cook for another 10 minutes.

SUPER EASY FRENCH FRIES

You're going to read this recipe and scoff, but I suggest you not rush to judgment. You also won't believe me when I tell you French fries made this way absorb less fat than doing them the standard way.

All that aside, just do what I say, and you won't be disappointed.

For 4-6

Pour 2½ cups of vegetable oil into a skillet, and stir in 2 pounds of potatoes cut into strips. That's right, you put the potatoes into UNHEATED oil.

Turn the heat to medium-high, and cook for 30 minutes or until they are as dark as you like. Drain them on some paper towels and that's it!

SMASHED ROASTED POTATOES

There's a little restaurant in Uruguay that you will probably never patronize. It has been described as the best seaside restaurant on the planet, and it is called La Huella (pronounced La WAY-shuh). I can't say it's worth the price of the trip just to eat there, especially since I am about to give you one of their best recipes, but after eating these potatoes you might want to consider it. They are best made over a hot charcoal grill, but your home oven will turn them out as well.

Note: Another way to make these is to first cook them in water until they are almost tender, make a little cross on top with a knife, and smash them. Then put on the butter or oil, and bake them at 450 degrees until they are nice and brown. This method makes sure the potatoes will be cooked enough since sizes vary so much.

For 4

4 medium-sized red-skinned or Yukon Gold potatoes

2 tbs. coarse salt

Freshly ground pepper

1/3 cup extra virgin olive oil

Preheat your oven to 350 degrees, and wrap each potato in foil. I usually don't wrap potatoes in foil but this is an exception. Place the potatoes on the oven rack and bake until tender, about 1 hour or a little more. If you pull them out and they are still a little hard, remove the foil and microwave them for about 5 minutes.

Place the potatoes on a baking sheet. Pour a little oil on them, and turn so they are coated all over. Press gently until the potato starts to cave a little. You want it slightly flattened to about half its original height, and broken up so that some of the flesh is showing. Pour some more oil on them, or substitute the oil with a large pat of butter. That's what I recommend. Do the same with the rest of the potatoes.

Season with salt and pepper, and drizzle about half the oil over them. Turn the oven up to 500 degrees, and roast them for about 30 minutes. They should be crispy and golden brown. If you need to, put them under the broiler for a few minutes. Drizzle with the rest of the oil. I like to add a little butter on top.

These potatoes are also wonderful covered with beef stew, cream chipped beef or any other filling you use on stuffed baked potatoes.

"PAN-BROWNED POTATOES

After you taste these potatoes, you might never use the oven to make oven-browned potatoes. They're wonderful with just about any main dish.

For 4

12 "baby" red potatoes

6 tablespoons butter

4 tablespoons water

Peel potatoes, place in small frying pan with butter and water. Bring to simmer and cover. Cook gently for 1 hour, tossing frequently as they brown. The water will be absorbed, and the potatoes will come out with a crisp, buttery skin, and fluffy on the inside.

COLCANNON

Since I gave you Bubble and Squeak, a traditional English dish, it only seems fair to give you one from Ireland as well. In Ireland, a heaped portion is served on each plate. A well is made in the center to hold a very generous amount of butter. The colcannon is eaten from around the edges, with each forkful being dipped into the melted butter. You can add almost any combination of greens, spinach, parsley, kale, or cabbage. I think kale is the most authentic. The right percentage is the greens should equal half the bulk of the potatoes.

For <u>4</u>

4 large russet potatoes, peeled, and quartered

1 lb. greens (about 1 tightly packed cup), chopped

2 scallions, chopped

½ cup half and half

8 tablespoons unsalted butter (or more)

Cook potatoes until they are fork-tender, drain well, return to pot, cover, salt, and let sit for 5 minutes. Remove cover, add 3 tablespoons of the butter, and break up potatoes with a fork. Add milk and, with an electric mixer, beat the potatoes until they are light and fluffy. Don't beat too long or they will become gummy.

While the potatoes are cooking, sauté the greens and scallions in 2 tablespoons of butter until they begin to wilt. Add to potatoes and mix well. Return to stove, turn off the heat, and cover for 3 minutes

When you serve, don't forget to add plenty of butter to the well in the middle. This is a great side dish with just about any kind of meat, chicken or fish.

HASSELBACH POTATOES

Another fun dish to lure you into the kitchen and impress some guests. A specialty of the Hasselbachen Hotel & Restaurant in Stockholm, Sweden, they can best be described as the Swedish version of baked potatoes. You can also make this dish with sweet potatoes.

The result is sort of a potato "fan" that looks spectacular.

For 2

2 large russet or Yukon Gold potatoes

¼ cup bread crumbs (store-bought are fine)

4 tablespoons grated Parmesan cheese

1 tablespoon butter

1 teaspoon paprika

3 tablespoons olive oil

Salt and pepper to taste

Pre-heat oven to 450 degrees, and oil a large baking dish.

In a small saucepan, over very low heat, melt the butter and add the bread crumbs, salt, pepper, Parmesan cheese, and paprika. Stir until well-mixed, and remove from heat.

Wash the potatoes and dry with some paper towels. Arrange 2 chopsticks or skewers on each side (this is to prevent you from cutting through the potato). Slice the potatoes thinly across. Drizzle potatoes with olive oil, carefully bending them to separate the sections so that the oil penetrates down through the slices.

Roll the top of a potato in the crumb mixture, and place in the baking dish. Repeat with other potato. Cover the baking dish with foil, and bake for 1 hour. Remove the foil, and continue baking until browned.

SCALLOPED POTATOES BAKED IN CREAM

This recipe is for those who want to take scalloped potatoes to the next level. They're way beyond regular scalloped potatoes, and one of the reasons is the use of cream rather than milk.

The leftovers freeze well and it's also a good show-off dish for entertaining.

For 4-6

1½–2 cups **_each_** of heavy cream and half and half

1 large clove of garlic, mashed with a mortar and pestle

Salt and freshly ground pepper, white preferably

1 bay leaf

5 peeled russet potatoes, sliced thinly

3–4 tablespoons of grated cheese, cheddar or Swiss

In a heavy saucepan with a cover, pour 1½ cups each of the cream and half and half. Stir in the garlic, a ½ teaspoon salt, a few grinds of pepper, and the bay leaf. Slice the potatoes evenly, 1/8-inch thick, dropping them as sliced into the cream. When all are in, add more cream if necessary to cover the potatoes by a ½ inch.

Bring the mixture to below the simmer, cover, and maintain at just below the simmer for 1 hour or up to 1½ hours. Check the potatoes frequently to make certain they are not bubbling, or the cream will curdle.

Transfer the potatoes and their liquid to a buttered, shallow baking and serving dish, and sprinkle the cheese on top. Bake at 425 degrees for 20 to 30 minutes, until the dish is bubbling and lightly browned on top. Rest the dish for 20 minutes, and serve.

FRIED TOMATOES WITH TOMATO CREAM GRAVY

Among just plain folks, fried green tomatoes were famous before the book and the movie. However, your choices shouldn't be limited to the green variety. I like fried red tomatoes better, and my favorite is fried yellow tomatoes with tomato gravy. Whatever color appeals to you, pick firm tomatoes so they hold up to the heat.

For 2

2-3 large ripe but firm tomatoes, sliced ½-inch thick

1 cup evaporated milk, or plain milk if that's all you have

2 tablespoons butter

1 tablespoon olive oil

Safflower oil for frying

¼ cup flour, divided use

2 cups cornmeal

¼ cup heavy cream

1 cup chicken broth

Freshly ground pepper (a generous amount)

Slice the tomatoes as directed but save all the odd pieces and the ends. Cut around the core pieces on the ends and cut into a coarse dice. Take one of the slices and do the same.

Heat the butter and olive oil in a skillet over medium heat. Add the diced tomatoes and cook until the mixture becomes soft, about 10 minutes. Add 2 tablespoons of the flour, stir, and cook for another 2 minutes, and add the chicken broth and cream. Cook until the gravy thickens, and set aside. Clean skillet, and heat enough cooking oil, over medium heat, to a depth of ½-inch, over medium heat.

Mix the cornmeal with the remaining flour, and add salt and pepper. Dip the tomato slices in the milk, letting the excess drip off and dredge them in the flour/cornmeal mixture, making sure they are well coated.

Fry the tomato slices until they are browned on both sides, about 5 minutes. Remove and drain on paper towels. The tomatoes can be kept warm in a 200-degree oven for 15 to 20 minutes. When ready to serve, place the tomatoes on a plate, and spoon the gravy on top.

This gravy is also great on mashed potatoes or biscuits.

SAUTEED BROCCOLI AND GARLIC

This recipe couldn't be any easier. I use it to go with an entrée that is a little complicated, so I don't spend all my time doing prep work.

For 2

½ head broccoli, florets only

2 cloves garlic, sliced very thin lengthwise

3 tablespoons olive oil

In a pot of boiling, salted water, parboil the florets until they are crisp-tender, about 5 to 6 minutes. Test them in 4 minutes because you don't want them to get soft. Drain well.

Heat the oil in a skillet over medium heat, and sauté the garlic slices for 1 minute, stirring frequently. Add the broccoli, and toss with the garlic for another 3 to 4 minutes. Remove from heat and serve.

NOTE: Once the dish is done, you can keep it indefinitely until you are ready to serve. Just microwave for 1 minute on high to heat it.

INCREDIBLE BAKED BEANS

Move over Boston, because these beans will give yours a run for your money. Try them, and you won't ever make them from scratch again. They are wonderful, and a great way to feed a crowd.

<u>**For 4**</u>

1 large can (1 lb., 2 oz.) of Campbell's pork and beans (don't buy cheap canned beans)

3 slices bacon, chopped

1 green pepper, chopped

1 small onion, chopped

1 tablespoon brown sugar

1 teaspoon chili powder

½ cup catsup

½ cup water

1 small jalapeño, chopped fine

Mix everything together in a 1½-quart casserole uncovered, and bake in a 250-degree oven for 3 hours.

Stir often. I promise these beans will be a big hit.

VEGETABLE FRITTERS

Quite often, when I buy vegetables, broccoli, zucchini, spinach, and cauliflower for instance, I have more than I want to make for a meal. Here's a wonderful solution to that problem – make fritters!

Basically, you are making an egg, flour, and milk batter, adding the vegetable, and dropping it into some hot oil, much like a pancake. I've found that adding about a quarter cup of grated Parmesan cheese does wonders for the flavor. You want the batter about the consistency of pancake batter.

Grate or chop the vegetables, and add them to the batter. In the case of broccoli, you might have to steam it a little first to get it tender. The first time I tried this, it was with a batch of broccoli slaw, those packages of julienned broccoli you find in the salad section of most supermarkets.

Drop the fritters into the hot oil, and fry on both sides until they are nicely browned. You can serve them plain, with sour cream, or maybe a little apple sauce.

Just to get you started, here's a recipe for Zucchini Fritters

You can't have too many recipes for zucchini, especially if you or your neighbors grow them. They are the rabbits of the vegetable kingdom.

This is a recipe from the south of France; the fritters are so good that even if you don't have too much zucchini, it's worth going out and buying some.

For 4

2 medium zucchinis, grated, salted, and placed in a colander to drain for 1 hour

⅔ cup flour

1 clove garlic, minced

1 teaspoon dried thyme

3 tablespoons grated Parmesan cheese

1 egg, separated

4 tablespoons water

1 tablespoon olive oil

4 tablespoons cooking oil

Salt and pepper

Rinse the grated zucchini, and gently squeeze dry with paper towels. Put the flour in a bowl, and make a well in the center. Add the egg yolk and 2 tablespoons water, and mix well, gradually incorporating the flour.

Add more water to make a smooth batter, about the consistency of pancake batter. Set aside for 30 minutes.

NOTE: It will save some time if you grate the zucchini, salt it, and while it's draining in the colander, whip up the batter. Meanwhile, beat the egg white until stiff.

Fold the zucchini into the batter, followed by the egg white. Using a 1/3-cup measure, spoon the batter into a skillet in which you have heated the safflower or canola oil over medium-high heat. Fry the fritters for 2 to 3 minutes on each side until they are golden brown. Drain on paper towels, and keep warm in a 200-degree oven until the batch is done. Serve as a side dish with almost anything.

SWEET POTATO & BANANA CASSEROLE

When I first met Lynne, she called me on Thanksgiving morning and asked me for a recipe she could contribute. She didn't cook a lot and she wanted to surprise her family.

The recipe is great with roast turkey, but can also be used with roast duck or pork. If you can make it so that people know there is something besides sweet potatoes in it, but can't tell what, you have succeeded.

For 4-6

3 medium sweet potatoes

2 very ripe bananas

2 teaspoons brown sugar

4 tablespoons butter

¼ cup orange juice

Salt and pepper

Peel the sweet potatoes, and cut them into large chunks. Boil in salted water until they are tender, and drain.

Peel bananas, and cut into 2-inch slices. Put the banana, brown sugar, and the sweet potatoes in a large bowl, and mash slightly with a fork. Add butter and orange juice and, using a hand mixer, beat at high speed until the mixture light and creamy. Bake at 350 degrees for 30 minutes.

GREEN BEANS & CASHEWS IN BROWN BUTTER SAUCE

This is a very simple way to enjoy green beans. You must make certain the beans are not overdone, and remain a little crisp. Another way I like them is just with a lot of salt sprinkled on top.

1 cup fresh green beans per serving

2-3 tablespoons butter

¼ cup cashews per serving

Trim and cook the green beans until a little crisp, and set aside. Melt the butter over moderate heat, and add the cashews. Sauté until they turn slightly brown, and add the beans. Turn the heat up to medium-high, and toss the mixture until the butter starts to turn slightly brown. Add salt to taste, and serve immediately.

HARVARD BEETS

These beets have absolutely nothing to do with Harvard other than their color. They are one of Lynne's favorites, maybe because her grandfather attended Harvard as an undergrad, and then graduated from Harvard Medical School.

NOTE: No one can tell the difference if canned or fresh beets are used so I highly recommend canned.

For 2

1 can quartered or whole beets, drained

¼ cup sugar

1 teaspoon cornstarch

¼ cup vinegar

1 tablespoon butter

Combine the sugar, cornstarch, and vinegar in a small pot, and bring to a gentle boil. Cook for 2 minutes, pour the beets in and stir. Just before serving, stir in the butter.

NOTE: You can substitute ¼ cup orange juice and a ½ tablespoon lemon juice in place of the vinegar, which will give you Yale Beets I suppose.

CREAMED CARROTS & MUSHROOMS IN A DILL SAUCE

Sometimes you just want a different take on vegetable and this recipe will give that to you. It's quite delicious and easy to make. Pretty also.

For 2

½ lb. mushrooms, sliced

3 medium carrots, peeled and sliced into ¼-inch rounds (it's okay to use canned carrots)

½ cup half and half

1 tablespoon flour

2 tablespoons butter

2 tablespoons dried dill weed

Salt and pepper

Cook the carrots in boiling, salted water until they are crisp-tender. Sauté the mushrooms in the butter until they just begin to give up their juices. Add the flour, and stir for 1 minute. Remove pan from heat, and stir in the half and half. Return to heat, and stir until the sauce gets thick and smooth. Add carrots and dill, and adjust seasoning with salt and pepper. Keep warm over very low heat until you are ready to serve. If the sauce is too thick, thin it with additional half and half.

OTHER STUFF

CHEF ED'S "KISS MY ASS" CHILI

Chili was introduced into the United States by Mexicans. They were mostly poor, and the only meat they could afford to raise was goat. Using their incredible knowledge of peppers, they made the tough leg meat of the goat tender by using chili peppers to break it down to slurry. They ate it with beans and tortillas.

Fast forward and what we have today are countless "chili cook-offs" featuring a bunch of one-dish cooks, mostly men, who go into a kitchen once a year and pretend to be chefs. Having no cooking skills to speak of, they have covered up their lack of knowledge by creating a mystique around chili that is just so much hogwash. "Never make it with beans." "Never use ground beef, always chunks." "No tomatoes." And of course, they all have secret ingredients, like road kill, that only they know about.

This is my chili. It has never won an award, it contains tomato products and hamburger, and, worst of all, it contains beans—lots of beans. Unlike those "masculine" recipes I mentioned, I've made it a little soupy, so the crackers you crunch into it don't stand up straight like pieces of *a* demolished building. I don't try to test your manhood, or womanhood for that matter, by making it so hot and spicy you can't eat it. I pass a bottle of Tabasco around and you can be as manly, or womanly, as you wish. It's very good chili, folks, and I urge you to try it.

For 4-6

1 ½ lbs. ground chuck

2 cups onions, chopped

¾ cup red peppers, seeds and ribs removed and diced

1 large jalapeno pepper, seeds and ribs removed and diced

2 cloves garlic, minced

1 small can diced mild green chilies

2 cans Bush's Chili Beans in mild sauce

2 tablespoons (or more) good chili powder—Gephardt's, for instance

½ tablespoon paprika

¼ teaspoon ground coriander

¼ teaspoon ground cumin

¼ teaspoon dried cilantro

1 4.5-oz can tomato sauce

1 can beef broth

1 can beer

2 tablespoons olive oil

Salt and freshly ground pepper

Put the beef, onions, peppers, garlic, and jalapeño in a large bowl, and mix it thoroughly with your hands. In a heavy cast-iron skillet, heat 2 tablespoons olive oil and add the meat mixture. With a large spoon, toss it around for 2 minutes, pat it down flat with the bottom of the spoon, turn the heat to medium, and cover. Cook for 5 minutes, mix it around some more, pat it down, cover, and cook for 5 more minutes. Do this 2 more times, uncover, and cook for another 5 minutes to evaporate some of the moisture.

Add the spices and beer, turn heat up to high, and reduce the broth slightly for about 5 minutes. Add the tomato sauce, green chilies, and beef broth, turn the heat to low, and simmer for 1 hour. Adjust seasonings and serve. It's better the next day, but I can never wait.

NOTE: While the chili is simmering, a skin, caused by fat, will appear on the surface. You can take your spoon and skim as much of this off as you like.

CINCINATTI CHILI

This chili is much different than what you're used to, and has some unusual applications and a much different history.

It was first served in Cincinnati in 1922. They still have Cincinnati chili parlors around the Midwest, and there is a small chain, Skyline Chili, in various parts of the country that serves Cincinnati Chili. I believe it has Greek origins and is also the basis for the chili in the original Coney Island hotdog.

I did a little research and discovered a mail order source called the Hard Times Café. Their chili tastes so authentic that even the mayor of Cincinnati said it compared favorably. You can find them on the Internet at www. hardtimes.com. A single package seasons five pounds of meat, but it has 2 packets of spice mix, so you don't have to make it all at once. It also freezes extremely well.

I must warn you, if you try it once, you will become addicted. Especially if you try the five-way deal: a layer of thin spaghetti, covered with a layer of chili, covered with a layer of kidney beans, covered with a layer of shredded Cheddar, then topped with diced onions.

BREAD PUDDING

Bread pudding is simply half and half or cream, mixed with sugar and eggs, usually a little vanilla extract, and some bread, and sometimes fruit added.

In this recipe, I use raisin bread, but you can also use croissants or any firm white bread. Be sure and butter the pieces well.

For 2-3

1 cup of fresh berries (blueberry, raspberries, blackberries, strawberries – or mix them up)

5-6 slices of cinnamon raisin bread cut into quarters

¼ cup softened butter

1 cup sugar

2 teaspoons vanilla extract

1 small carton of half and half

6 large eggs, beaten

Lay the bread slices directly on the middle rack of your oven, which has been pre-heated to 375 degrees. Toast for 10 minutes, and remove the slices, but leave the oven on.

Whisk the eggs and half and half together with the sugar, until the sugar has completely dissolved. Add the vanilla extract a stir well.

Take the bread out of the oven and butter each slice with a heavy layer of soft butter. Cut into quarters.

Arrange layers of the bread neatly in a shallow baking dish (about 8x12), or in a deep soufflé dish, and sprinkle with some blueberries. Continue the layering and finish with a layer of blueberries. Pour the egg mixture over all. Place the baking dish in a large dish with about 1 inch of water in it. Bake for 45 minutes, and test with a toothpick. If it does not come out clean, bake another 15 minutes. Remove from oven, and let rest for 1 hour. The pudding will continue to bake after it's removed from the oven.

CHOCOHOLICS HEAVEN

Chocolate tastes great and is good for you so what's not to like? If you like chocolate as much as I do, here's a treat that will only please you if you turn a blind eye to the calorie situation.

4 tablespoons chocolate syrup

1 cup chocolate milk

2 cups chocolate ice cream

Mix everything well in a blender until smooth, and enjoy. Serve with Oreo Cookies.

FRITO PIE

Chances are, if you ever attended a high school football game in Texas, you've eaten a Frito Pie. In the realm of gourmet cooking, it's not much, but, in the realm of junk food, it's a classic. Be careful, it's also addictive

For 1

1 small bag of Fritos

Chili of your choice (I like Hormel without beans)

Shredded cheddar cheese

Chopped onions (optional)

Pour the Fritos into a wide bowl, or anything else that's handy. Heat the chili and add a generous portion (it should pretty much cover the Fritos), and then sprinkle some cheddar cheese on top. Add onions if you want them.

NOTE: The traditional way of eating this is to just open the bag and pour in the chili and cheese, and onions if they're using them. I predict that once you try this dish you'll repeat it often.

A PLOUGHMAN'S LUNCH WITH PUB ONIONS

This is a little project that will make cooking almost fun, especially if you have a partner to share it with. Actually, no cooking is involved, just a little assembly and some patience.

You can find this lunch in almost every English or Irish pub. It's a simple meal of smoked sausage or kielbasa, crusty bread, and big chunks of cheddar cheese, and it's always served with a generous helping of pickled pub onions. It was one of our best sellers in my deli, Let's Do Lunch!

You can use other kinds of hard cheese such as Roquefort or Gouda, but I think aged cheddar goes best with it. I had a hard time finding pickled pub onions, so I decided to make my own. According to my customers, they were better than the commercial ones, and are very simple to make.

First, buy a jar of pickled onions (the small ones they use for Gibson Cocktails). They can be found in just about any supermarket. Empty the jar of any liquid, fill it to the brim with balsamic vinegar, and let the onions marinate for a day or two on a shelf. Once they are marinated, you can keep them in the fridge, and they will last for several months. They're also very good with sandwiches.

All you need to complete the lunch is the cheese, sausage, and bread cut into large chunks. You won't believe how delicious the onions are as a perfect mate to the rest of the lunch.

To be correct, you should have a pint of beer or ale along with the lunch.

POPOVERS

These were once known as Laplanders and I haven't a clue as to why. For years, you were told to pre-heat the oven to very high, put them in, and reduce the heat after twenty minutes. Then, I suppose, someone lost track of time, forgot to pre-heat the oven, and just put them in the cold oven. It worked even better.

You will need a muffin pan.

For 4

2 eggs

1 cup of sifted flour

1 teaspoon salt

1 cup milk

2 tablespoons melted butter

Beat the eggs lightly, and add the flour and salt. Beat for 1 minute, and add the milk. Stir to make a smooth batter, and add the melted butter. The less you beat the batter, the better.

Take a piece of butter in a paper towel and rub on the bottom and sides of the muffin cups. Fill the cups with batter up to about two thirds full. Place in a cold oven set for 425 degrees, and bake 30 to 35 minutes. Do not open the oven door for 20 minutes. Reduce the temperature if the popovers seem to be getting too brown.

You can pierce the puffs with a fork to dry them out a little, if you like. With my family, they never last long enough to worry about that.

NOTE: You have just received a two-in-one cooking lesson. This is the same recipe you use for Yorkshire pudding. Just pour it in the baking pan you used to roast beef and pop it in a 350-degree oven for 20 minutes.

Made in the USA
Las Vegas, NV
13 December 2020